BOOK 1
AQA GCSE ENGLISH LANGUAGE

ESTABLISHING THE SKILLS FOR LEARNING AND ASSESSMENT

Helen Backhouse
Beverley Emm

OXFORD
UNIVERSITY PRESS

CONTENTS

AQA GCSE English Language specification overview

The exam papers

The grade you receive at the end of your AQA GCSE English Language course is entirely based on your performance in two exam papers. The following provides a summary of these two exam papers:

Exam paper	Reading and Writing questions and marks	Assessment Objectives	Timing	Marks (and % of GCSE)
Paper 1: Explorations in Creative Reading and Writing	**Section A: Reading** Exam text: • One unseen literature fiction text Exam questions and marks: • One short form question (1 x 4 marks) • Two longer form questions (2 x 8 marks) • One extended question (1 x 20 marks)	Reading: • AO1 • AO2 • AO4	1 hour 45 minutes	Reading: 40 marks (25% of GCSE) Writing: 40 marks (25% of GCSE) Paper 1 total: 80 marks (50% of GCSE)
	Section B: Writing Descriptive or narrative writing Exam question and marks: • One extended writing question (24 marks for content, 16 marks for technical accuracy)	Writing: • AO5 • AO6		
Paper 2: Writers' Viewpoints and Perspectives	**Section A: Reading** Exam text: • One unseen non-fiction text and one unseen literary non-fiction text Exam questions and marks: • One short form question (1 x 4 marks) • Two longer form questions (1 x 8 marks and 1 x 12 marks) • One extended question (1 x 16 marks)	Reading: • AO1 • AO2 • AO3	1 hour 45 minutes	Reading: 40 marks (25% of GCSE) Writing: 40 marks (25% of GCSE) Paper 2 total: 80 marks (50% of GCSE)
	Section B: Writing Writing to present a viewpoint Exam question and marks: • One extended writing question (24 marks for content, 16 marks for technical accuracy)	Writing: • AO5 • AO6		

The Assessment Objectives (AOs)

Assessment Objectives are the skills that underpin all qualifications. Your GCSE English Language exam papers are testing six Assessment Objectives – AOs 1-6 – whilst your Spoken Language tests AOs 7-9.

The following table outlines the Assessment Objectives for GCSE English Language and the exam paper questions where each Assessment Objective is tested:

Assessment Objective (AO)		Paper 1	Paper 2
AO1	• Identify and interpret explicit and implicit information and ideas	Question 1	Question 1
	• Select and synthesise evidence from different texts	-	Question 2
AO2	Explain, comment on and analyse how writers use language and structure to achieve effects and influence readers, using relevant subject terminology to support their views	Question 2 Question 3	Question 3
AO3	Compare writers' ideas and perspectives, as well as how these are conveyed, across two or more texts	-	Question 4
AO4	Evaluate texts critically and support this with appropriate textual references	Question 4	-
AO5	Communicate clearly, effectively and imaginatively, selecting and adapting tone, style and register for different forms, purposes and audiences. Organise information and ideas, using structural and grammatical features to support coherence and cohesion of texts	Question 5	Question 5
AO6	Candidates must use a range of vocabulary and sentence structures for clarity, purpose and effect, with accurate spelling and punctuation.	Question 5	Question 5
AO7	Demonstrate presentation skills in a formal setting	n/a	n/a
AO8	Listen and respond appropriately to spoken language, including to questions and feedback on presentations	n/a	n/a
AO9	Use spoken Standard English effectively in speeches and presentations.	n/a	n/a

What sorts of texts and stimulus tasks will the exam papers include?

Paper 1

Section A: Reading will include the following types of text:

- A prose literature text from either the 20th or 21st century
- It will be an extract from a novel or short story.
- It will focus on openings, endings, narrative perspectives and points of view, narrative or descriptive passages, character, atmospheric descriptions and other appropriate narrative and descriptive approaches.

Section B: Writing will include the following stimulus:

- There will be a choice of scenario, either a written prompt or a visual image related to the topic of the reading text in Section A. The scenario sets out a context for writing with a designated audience, purpose and form that will differ to those specified in Paper 2.
- You will produce your own writing, inspired by the topic that you responded to in Section A.

Paper 2

Section A: Reading will include the following types of text:

- Two linked sources (one non-fiction and one literary non-fiction) from different time periods (one 19th century and one from either the 20th or 21st century, depending on the time period of the text in Paper 1) and different genres in order to consider how each presents a perspective or viewpoint to influence the reader.

Section B: Writing will include the following stimulus:

- You will produce a written text to a specified audience, purpose and form in which you give your own perspective on the theme that has been introduced in Section A.

Spoken Language

As well as preparing for the two GCSE English Language exams, your course also includes Spoken Language assessment. This is **not** an exam. Instead your teacher sets and marks the assessments.

There are three separate Assessment Objectives covering Spoken Language – AO7, AO8 and AO9. At the end of your course you will receive a separate endorsement for Spoken Language, which means it will not count as part of your GCSE English Language qualification.

Introduction to this book

How this book will help you

Develop your reading and writing skills

The primary aim of this book is to develop and improve your reading and writing skills. Crucially however, in this book, you will be doing this in the context of what the exam papers will be asking of you at the end of your course. So, the skills you will be practising throughout this book are ideal preparation for your two English Language exam papers.

Explore the types of texts that you will face in the exams

In your English Language exams you will have to respond to a number of unseen texts. In order to prepare you fully for the range and types of text that you might face in the exam, this book is structured thematically so you can explore the connections between texts. This is ideal preparation for your exams as the unseen texts in your exam papers will be of different types (fiction and non-fiction), from different historical periods (from the 19th, 20th and 21st centuries) and will in some instances be connected.

Become familiar with the Assessment Objectives and exam paper requirements

Assessment Objectives are the skills that underpin all qualifications. Your GCSE English Language exam papers are testing six Assessment Objectives (see pages 4 and 5). Chapters 1 to 5 of this book take exactly the same approach – each chapter develops your reading and writing skills addressing the same Assessment Objectives. This revisiting of Assessment Objectives and supported practising of tasks, in different thematic contexts and with different texts, will ensure that your skills improve and that you're in the best possible position to start your exam preparation. Chapter 6 pulls together all the skills that you have been practising in order to help prepare you for 'mock' exam papers at the end of the book.

Monitor progress through assessments

Chapters 1 to 5 in this book include end of chapter assessments that enable you to demonstrate what you have learnt and help your teacher assess your progress. Each of these assessments includes tasks that prepare you for the types of task that you will be facing in your GCSE English Language exams. The sample papers at the end of the book give you the opportunity to bring together all that you have been learning and practising in a 'mock' exam situation.

A note on spelling

Certain words, for example 'synthesize' and 'organize', have been spelt with 'ize' throughout this book. It is equally acceptable to spell these words and others with 'ise'.

How is the book structured?

Chapters 1 to 5

Chapters 1 to 5 develop your reading and writing skills within different themes. Each chapter opens with an introductory page that introduces the theme, explains the skills you will be developing and includes an introductory activity.

Each chapter then includes a range of fiction, non-fiction and literary non-fiction texts, from different historical periods, to help you develop your reading skills. Each chapter covers all the same reading Assessment Objectives and across the chapters you will encounter all of the text types from all of the historical periods that your exam paper texts will be taken from at the end of your course.

Your writing skills are also developed throughout every chapter including a focus on improving your technical accuracy (or SPAG – Spelling, Punctuation And Grammar). This is done in the context of the chapter to help embed these vital skills into your writing.

Chapter 6

Chapter 6 pulls all of the skills together that you have learnt throughout the course, revisiting key points and providing you with revision practise. The chapter and book concludes with exam–style questions, to enable you and your teacher to see how much progress you have made.

What are the main features within this book?

 ### Activities

To develop your reading responses to the wide range of texts included in this book as well as developing your writing skills, you will find activities all linked to the types of question you will face in your exams. The source texts reflect the types of text that you will face in your two exams.

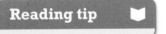 ### Tips, Key terms and glossed words

These features help support your understanding of key terms, concepts and more difficult words within a source text. These therefore enable you to concentrate fully on developing your exam response skills.

Progress check

In addition to the summative end of chapter assessments, you will also find regular formative assessments in the form of 'Progress checks'. These enable you to establish whether through peer or self-assessment how confident you feel about what you have been learning.

Further GCSE English Language and English Literature student resources

AQA GCSE English Language Student Book 2: Assessment Preparation for Paper 1 and Paper 2

Student Book 2 provides students with all the exam preparation and practice that students need to succeed. The book is divided into Reading and Writing sections which guide students through the exam questions. The book features:

- a range of texts similar to those students will encounter in the exam
- marked sample student responses at different levels
- opportunities for self-assessment and peer-assessment
- advice on how students can improve their responses
- sample exam papers.

AQA GCSE English Language Revision Workbook Targeting Grade 5 and Targeting Grades 6 to 9

These write-in workbooks, structured around the individual exam questions, help students achieve grades 5 to 9 by taking active control of their revision. Ideal for use in school or at home, the workbooks:

- guide students through the exam papers and the individual questions
- provide extensive practice opportunities, revision tips and specification guidance
- engage and motivate through the full colour design and targeted support
- feature self-evaluation checklists and regular formative assessment opportunities
- include sample responses and full sample exam papers.

AQA GCSE English Literature Student Book

This Student Book provides in-depth skills development for the English Literature specification, including:

- comprehensive coverage and practice of the poetry anthology and unseen poetry requirements
- advice and activities to support Shakespeare, the 19th-century novel and modern prose and drama
- sample student responses at different levels and sample exam-style tasks to help prepare you for the exam paper questions
- Stretch and Support features to ensure all students make progress
- clear, student-friendly explanations of the Assessment Objectives and the skills required to meet them.

1 Bugs

**Cockroaches...
spiders...
grasshoppers...
snails.
You either love
them or you
hate them.**

Are you the sort of person whose skin crawls at the sight of a centipede with all those legs? Do bugs make you squirm?

Or do you really quite like them?

Some people are fascinated by bugs. They study them, keep them as pets and even eat them. Did you know Mexico has over 500 species of edible insects, and in Colombia, roasted large-bottomed ants (*hormigas culonas*) are a speciality?

In this chapter you will encounter many different attitudes to the insect world by reading a range of writing from different genres and times.

Activity

a Look at each image on this page and decide how you would rate it for 'likeability'. Choose from 1 to 5, with 5 being the most likeable.

b With a partner, discuss your experience of bugs and how you feel about them. Are there any that you like? Are there any that you hate? What are your reasons?

You might like to consider:

- bugs in movies and on TV
- apps and computer games involving bugs
- bugs you have seen on holiday
- childhood experiences of bugs.

Skills and Assessment Objectives

All the reading and writing skills in this chapter are linked to the Assessment Objectives (AOs) for GCSE English Language.

Reading skills include how to:

- find and interpret information and ideas
- find and summarize evidence from texts to support your views
- explain how writers use language for particular effects
- examine how writers organize texts for particular effects
- compare writers' ideas and attitudes
- make judgements about what a writer does to make a piece of writing effective.

Writing skills include how to:

- write imaginatively in different forms for particular purposes and readers
- organize your written ideas in a carefully crafted way.

woodlouse

Likeability factor?

spider

Likeability factor?

slug

Likeability factor?

scorpion

Likeability factor?

caterpillar

Likeability factor?

1 All creatures great and small

- To find and interpret information and ideas **(AO1)**
- To analyse how the writer uses rhetorical questions and emotive language to persuade others to agree with his point of view **(AO2)**

Many of us have seen the TV reality show *I'm A Celebrity… Get Me Out Of Here!*

We pity the poor celebrities doing their trials, but have you ever thought about the poor creatures involved? Chris Packham, a TV wildlife expert, is interviewed about this in the newspaper article below.

Extract from The Daily Mail website, December 2009

Autumnwatch presenter Chris Packham slams *I'm A Celebrity…* for 'killing animals and cruelty to bugs and insects'

TV wildlife expert Chris Packham has blasted *I'm A Celebrity… Get Me Out of Here!* for being cruel to bugs and insects. The host of BBC2's *Autumnwatch* […] says he is appalled by how the show's bosses and celebrities abuse animals in the Aussie outback.

5 The 48-year-old, who shot to fame on the BAFTA-winning BBC1 children's programme *The Really Wild Show,* says it is wrong that creatures are killed for entertainment purposes.

Chris told *Yours* magazine: 'The people working on *I'm A Celebrity… Get Me Out of Here!* have no regard for creatures' lives. If a celebrity trod on
10 a cat it would be on the front page of every newspaper but they jump up and down on as many cockroaches, spiders and bugs as they like. From the first series I've been nothing short of appalled by the way they abuse animals. What sickens me more than anything is when people say "But they're only insects." I happen to really like insects and more than
15 anything I like life.

'There's not a single living organism on this planet that wants to die [...]

'Other aspects of the programme like the physical trials can be entertaining but I don't find the treatment of creatures excusable at all. The insects are wriggling as they shove them into their mouths.

20 Surely they have feelings? They do have nervous systems – for example witchety grubs and mealworms shy away from heat.

'There is a lunatic divide whereby it's okay to slaughter as many bugs as we like but if it is anything cute and furry it immediately makes front page news. [...]

25 'If a celebrity were genuinely starving I'd have no problems with it. But when they are doing it for entertainment it's no more than exploitation.

'I'd like to see the animal aspects of the programme taken out. I'm sure there are enough brains in the programming department to come up with different challenges that are equally exciting but don't involve

30 killing creatures.'

Key terms

Explicit: clearly stated; you just need to find it

Implicit: suggested; you have to **interpret** the text to work it out for yourself

Interpret: explain the meaning of something in your own words, showing your understanding

The information and ideas contained in this article are both **explicit** and **implicit**. Make sure that you understand the difference by reading the sentence below.

Ellen's comment is explicit. She says that she is hungry.

'I'm hungry. A quick snack would help out,' said Ellen, looking at James's sweets.

Ellen's wish to eat James's sweets is implicit, suggested by what she says and where she looks.

Reading tip 📖

An easy way of finding explicit information is to choose facts stated in the article.

Activity 1

a Look at the first two paragraphs of the article on page 12. One explicit piece of information about Chris Packham is that he is a TV wildlife expert.

Find four other explicit pieces of information about him in this paragraph from the selection below. Choose the most straightforward facts that no one can argue with.

A He spoke to *Yours* magazine.

B He is extremely distressed.

C He never watches *I'm A Celebrity... Get Me Out Of Here!*

D He thinks TV makers are selfish.

E He is 48.

F He used to work on *The Really Wild Show.*

G He hosts BBC2's *Autumnwatch.*

H He thinks *I'm A Celebrity... Get Me Out of Here!* is abusive to animals and people.

b Paragraph two contains both explicit and implicit information on Packham's views about the treatment of insects. Use the sentence starters below to write about Packham's views.

Packham thinks that....

He also suggests that...

His words imply that he feels...

c In the rest of the article, Packham reveals more about his views on the treatment of creatures. List four more points he makes, using your own words where you can.

d Packham makes a positive comment about the programme and its makers to balance his views and suggest that he is reasonable. For example he says 'Other aspects of the programme like the physical trials can be entertaining...'. Find another example of a positive comment by Packham in this article.

Activity 2

Using all the work you have done so far, write your response to the following question:

> What do you understand about Chris Packham's views from the article? Use your own words and quotations to prove your points. Use explicit and implicit information in your answer.

Use the spider diagram below to help you plan your answer.

the people that make the programme

the treatment of creatures

the celebrities taking part

Chris Packham's views

the experience of the creatures

how the programme could be changed

people that watch it

Use the model below to structure your writing. The student makes a **point**, gives **evidence** from the text and then **explains** what that evidence shows.

Packham thinks that the programme-makers are cruel. ← point

He says 'I've been nothing short of appalled by the way they ← evidence
abuse animals'. This suggests that he is upset and disgusted — explanation
by the programme makers.

In the article on page 12, Packham uses **emotive language** to show his strong feelings about animal cruelty. He uses this language to persuade the reader to agree with him. The writer of this article also chooses emotive words to help the reader understand Packham's views.

Activity 3

a Look at the headline and the first two paragraphs (Lines 1–7). Find three examples of emotive words or phrases that show how strongly Packham feels. Record your examples in a table like the one started below, and explain the effect on the reader.

Emotive language	Effect
'appalled…'	The word 'appalled' suggests that Chris Packham is horrified by the way animals are treated in this TV programme.

b In Line 22–23, Chris Packam says: 'There is a lunatic divide whereby it's okay to slaughter as many bugs as we like'. What effect do the words 'lunatic divide' and 'slaughter' have on the reader? Add these examples to the table and include your ideas about effect.

c Look at any language used for emotive effect in the rest of the article. Select two more examples and explain the effect on the reader. Add your ideas to the table.

d Compare your table with a partner's. Discuss how the examples you have found show the strength of Chris Packham's feelings. Add any further points to your table following your discussion.

Another way Packham shows his strong feelings about animal cruelty is by using a **rhetorical question**. This asks readers a question and persuades them to agree with his views.

Activity 4

a Find the rhetorical question in the fifth paragraph.

b Explain how it encourages us to agree with Packham's views.

Activity 5

Using all the work you have done so far on emotive language and rhetorical questions, write your response to the following question:

> How does Packham use language to persuade people to agree with his point of view about the treatment of insects?

Remember to use the PEE (Point, Evidence, Explanation) structure in your answer. Plan your answer using a table like the one below.

Structure	Text
First point	In the article, one method that Packham uses to persuade readers to agree with him is...
Evidence	
Explanation	
Second point	A second method that Packham uses to persuade the readers to agree with his point of view is...
Evidence	
Explanation	

2 Obsession

Skills and objectives

- To evaluate how effectively the writer creates character and atmosphere **(AO4)**

Key term

Mood: the feeling or atmosphere created by a piece of writing

Writers need to create strong openings to grasp the reader's attention and keep them reading. With a short story, the opening must set the scene, launch the plot and establish the **mood** and characters. Things must happen quickly!

Here is the opening of a short story called 'The Snail Watcher' by Patricia Highsmith. It tells us as lot about the character of Mr Knoppert.

Extract from 'The Snail Watcher' by Patricia Highsmith

When Mr Peter Knoppert began to make a hobby of snail-watching, he had no idea that his handful of specimens would become hundreds in no time. Only two months after the original snails were carried up to the Knoppert study, some thirty glass tanks and bowls, all teeming with
5 snails, lined the walls, rested on the desk and windowsills, and were beginning even to cover the floor. Mrs Knoppert disapproved strongly, and would no longer enter the room. It smelled, she said, and besides she had once stepped on a snail by accident, a horrible sensation she would never forget. But the more his wife and friends deplored[1]
10 his unusual and vaguely repellent[2] pastime, the more pleasure Mr Knoppert seemed to find in it.

'I never cared for nature before in my life,' Mr Knoppert often remarked – he was a partner in a brokerage firm[3], a man who had devoted all his life to the science of finance – 'but snails have opened my eyes to the
15 beauty of the animal world.'

If his friends commented that snails were not really animals, and their slimy habitats hardly the best example of the beauty of nature, Mr Knoppert would tell them with a superior smile that they simply didn't know all that he knew about snails.

[1]deplored – disapproved of
[2]repellent – distasteful, will drive something away
[3]brokerage firm – a business that buys and sells stocks and shares

Activity 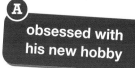 1

a Which of the following descriptions apply to Mr Knoppert at the start of the story?

A obsessed with his new hobby

B knows a lot about snails when he starts to collect them

C displays his snails throughout the house

D smug

E likes to be right all the time

F works as an accountant

G very odd

b Draw a spider diagram with 'Mr Knoppert' in the centre and write your chosen descriptions for him in the surrounding bubbles. Find quotations to support three of your chosen points.

c Compare your spider diagram with a partner's. Discuss your chosen descriptions, as well as your supporting quotations, to see if you agree.

d Mr Knoppert's wife and friends are also mentioned at the start of the story. With your partner, discuss what this detail adds to our understanding of Mr Knoppert.

As the story develops, the writer reveals more information about Mr Knoppert to interest the reader. Mr Knoppert's behaviour becomes odd and obsessive as he starts breeding the snails. In the following extract, the females have laid their eggs and Mr Knoppert waits for the baby snails to be born.

Extract from 'The Snail Watcher' by Patricia Highsmith

He had to go and look at the eggs every hour that he was at home. He looked at them every morning to see if any change had taken place and the eggs were his last thought every night before he went to bed. Moreover, another snail was now digging a pit. And another pair of
5   snails was mating! The first batch of eggs turned a greyish colour, and minuscule[1] spirals of shells became discernible[2] on one side of each egg. Mr Knoppert's anticipation rose to a higher pitch. At last a morning arrived – the eighteenth after laying, according to Mr Knoppert's careful count – when he looked down into the egg pit and saw the first tiny
10   moving head, the first stubby little antennae[3] uncertainly exploring the nest. Mr Knoppert was as happy as the father of a new child. Every one of the seventy or more eggs in the pit came miraculously to life. He had seen the entire reproductive cycle[4] evolve to a successful conclusion. And the fact that no one, at least no one that he knew of,
15   was acquainted[5] with a fraction of what he knew, lent his knowledge a thrill of discovery, the piquancy of the esoteric[6]. Mr Knoppert made notes on successive[7] matings and egg hatchings. He narrated snail biology to fascinated, more often shocked, friends and guests, until his wife squirmed with embarrassment.

[1]minuscule – tiny
[2]discernible – possible to see
[3]antennae – feeler
[4]reproductive cycle – sequence of events leading to birth
[5]acquainted – familiar
[6]piquancy of the esoteric – excitement of specialist knowledge
[7]successive – one after another

Activity 2

a In this extract, the writer includes details to develop Mr Knoppert's character. Find five details that you think show how obsessed Mr Knoppert has become. Write them down as quotations.

b Compare your list with a partner's. Agree the top three details that show Mr Knoppert's weird behaviour. Share these with the class.

Activity 3

Read the student response to the following question:

> How successful is Patricia Highsmith in conveying Mr Knoppert's growing obsession with snails? Give your own opinion and quote from both extracts to support what you say.

> I think Highsmith is pretty successful in showing Mr Knoppert's obsession. She shows he is pretty weird because he is counting the days until the eggs hatch, 'according to Mr Knoppert's careful count'. The word 'careful' shows that he is pretty weird.

a Identify the point, evidence and explanation in this response.

b Improve the written expression. Which words and phrases would you replace?

c Now write a second, well-written PEE paragraph to add a second point.

The writer also includes details to create a particular atmosphere. In 'The Snail Watcher', the snails continue to breed and eventually take over the study. At the end of the story, the writer creates a surreal atmosphere of horror as Mr Knoppert becomes trapped in the room.

Extract from 'The Snail Watcher' by Patricia Highsmith

He crawled to the door, heedless of the sea of snails he crushed under hands and knees. He could not get the door open. There were so many snails on it, crossing and re-crossing the crack of the door on all sides, they actually resisted his strength.

5 'Edna!' A snail crawled into his mouth. He spat it out in disgust. Mr Knoppert tried to brush the snails off his arms. But for every hundred he dislodged, four hundred seemed to slide upon him and fasten to him again, as if they deliberately sought him out as the only comparatively snail-free surface in the room. There were snails crawling over his eyes.

10 Then just as he staggered to his feet, something else hit him – Mr Knoppert couldn't even see what. He was fainting! At any rate, he was on the floor. His arms felt like leaden weights as he tried to reach his nostrils, his eyes, to free them from the sealing, murderous snail bodies.

'Help!' He swallowed a snail. Choking, he widened his mouth for air
15 and felt a snail crawl over his lips on to his tongue. He was in hell! He could feel them gliding over his legs like a glutinous river, pinning his legs to the floor. 'Ugh!' Mr Knoppert's breath came in feeble gasps. His vision grew black, a horrible, undulating black. He could not breathe at all, because he could not reach his nostrils, could not move his hands.

Activity 4

In a small group, discuss how the writer successfully creates an atmosphere of horror. Link the points below to the relevant quotations. The first one has been done for you.

Points	Quotations

Points

The writer uses verbs that show Mr Knoppert's attempts to remove the snails.

The writer uses verbs that show the snails' movements and actions.

The writer uses a simile to create a picture of the slimy setting.

The writer mentions parts of Mr Knoppert's body to show how he is powerless.

The writer uses speech to show Mr Knoppert's disgust.

The writer uses adjectives to describe the snails' actions and power.

The writer uses repetition to convey the horror of the situation.

Quotations

'Ugh!'

'murderous snail bodies'

'His arms… reach his nostrils, his eyes'

'There were snails crawling over his eyes'

'like a glutinous river'

'he could not reach his nostrils, could not move his hands.'

'He spat it out in disgust. Mr Knoppert tried to brush the snails off'

Activity 5

Now select one of the points above and write a PEE paragraph, adding the explanation to comment on how the writer creates an atmosphere of horror.

To remind yourself how to write a PEE paragraph, turn back to page 17.

3 Caught in the spider's web

Skills and objectives

- To communicate imaginatively, focusing in particular on creating character and atmosphere **(AO5)**

- To write clearly and accurately **(AO6)**

You are going to write an imaginative short story suggested by the picture below. Alternatively, you can use the text as a line in a short story – you could begin with it or lead up to it. You do not need to take the text or picture literally: 'suggested by' means you can use them as a starting point to stimulate your imagination.

> 'Something dark scuttled across the floor...'

Stage 1: Planning

Part 1: Consider an example

Before starting to write a narrative, you need to organize your thoughts. Look at the plan below for the story 'The Snail Watcher' featured in the last lesson.

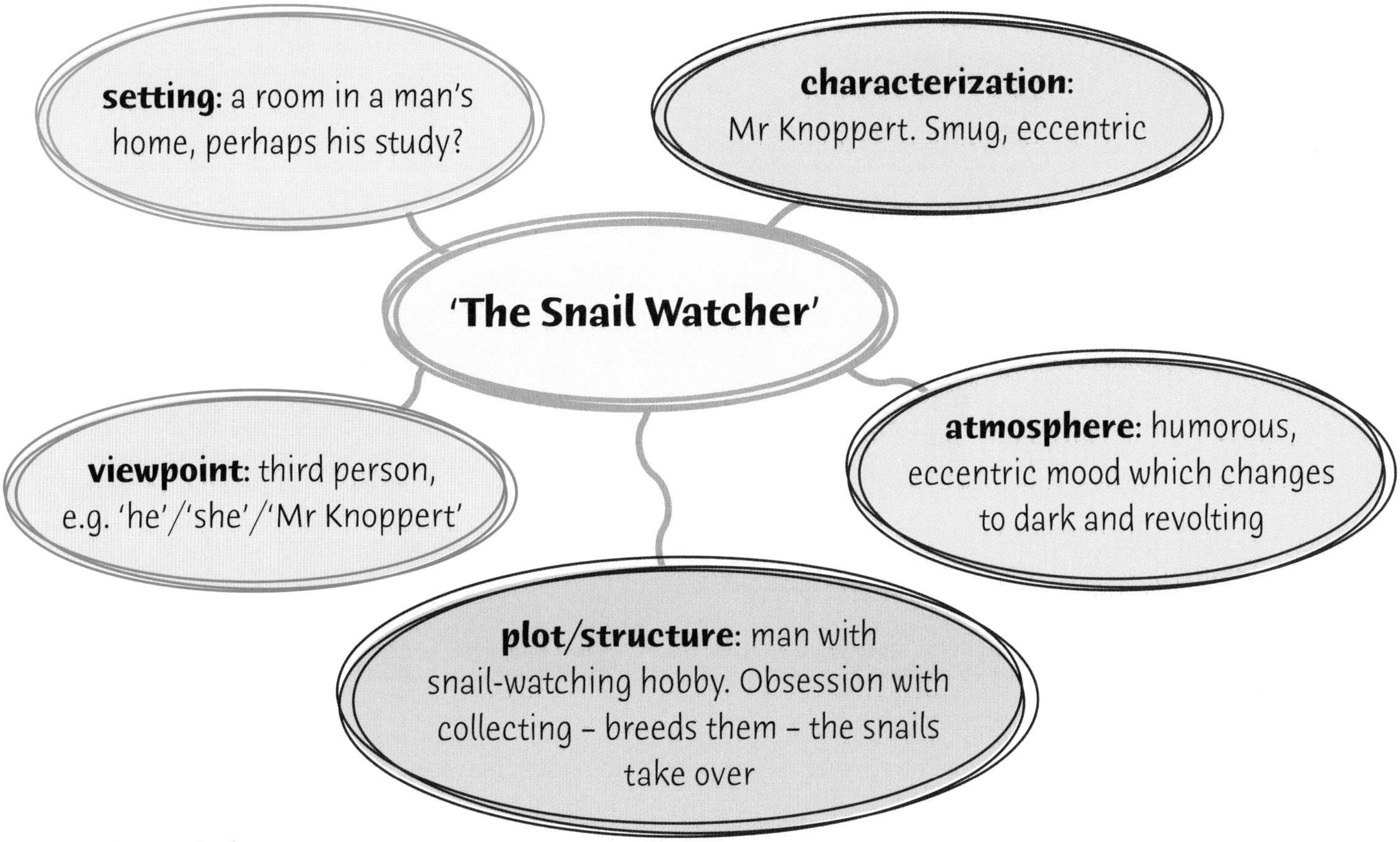

setting: a room in a man's home, perhaps his study?

characterization: Mr Knoppert. Smug, eccentric

'The Snail Watcher'

viewpoint: third person, e.g. 'he'/'she'/'Mr Knoppert'

atmosphere: humorous, eccentric mood which changes to dark and revolting

plot/structure: man with snail-watching hobby. Obsession with collecting – breeds them – the snails take over

Part 2: Apply it to your story

Activity 1

a Complete a similar plan for your own story. Use the points below to create a spider diagram to help you.

- Setting: Where and when will your story take place?
- Characterization: Who is the story about?
- Viewpoint: Who is telling the story? A first-person narrator (using *I, we*), or a third-person narrator (using *he/she/they/names*)
- Plot/structure: How will your story begin? What conflict will be encountered and how will it be resolved?
- Atmosphere: What mood do you want to create? Remember it can change as the story progresses.

b Discuss your notes with a partner, adding any ideas for improvement.

c Decide how much (if any) direct speech you want to use in your story. Jot down some ideas to try out your characters' voices. Dialogue should not make up more than a quarter of your story and must be laid out correctly.

Creating character

Activity 2

Examples

a With a partner, discuss the differences between the two paragraphs below. How does the use of detail included by the writer help to create very different impressions of Hannah?

Attracted by a sudden shout, Hannah looked out of the window. A young boy was trapped in the alley by a gang of youths. Hannah walked away from the window, slumped down into the sofa, turned up the sound on the TV and considered her perfectly painted nails. The thought of going outdoors to try to help was not on her agenda. She hated confrontation.

Attracted by a sudden shout, Hannah shot to the window. A young boy was trapped in the alley by a gang of youths. Hannah moved from the window, quickly slipped on her trainers and dashed outside. She didn't think about the potential danger. She just knew she had to intervene and help the boy.

Applying to your writing

b Decide how you want the reader to react to your main character and make a note of some details about them that will achieve this effect.

- Choose two physical features to mention that might suggest something about their personality.

- Choose two actions that might reveal something about your main character's personality.

Creating atmosphere

Activity 3

Examples

a With a partner, discuss the difference between the two paragraphs below. How do the details included by the writer help to create two very different atmospheres?

> It was night. Occasionally, the moon cast shadows across the empty house, but then it disappeared behind a cloud and everything was encased in darkness once more. Every now and again, Amy heard an owl hoot in the distance or saw the odd silhouette of a bat flutter by, but most of the time it was silent and still. Death hung in the air like an omen.

> It was a bright summer's day. Occasionally, a gentle breeze lifted the wind chimes and when the sun caught their shiny metal surface, glinting shafts of light were scattered across the grass. Amy could hear her family in the kitchen, laughing loudly and chattering away about lighting the barbecue, with Dad wearing one of those silly chef's hats. She smiled. On a day like this, she thought, life was good.

Applying to your writing

b Decide how you want the reader to feel throughout your story and make a note of some details that will achieve this atmosphere. You may want to vary your atmosphere at different stages in the story, for example, lulling your reader into a false sense of security just before a moment of shock or fear.

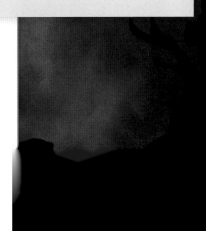

Stage 2: Writing

Writing tip

Remember to use paragraphs within your writing.

Aim to write a short story of six to eight paragraphs with a clear sense of beginning and end.

A new paragraph is needed to mark a change of:

- topic
- time
- place
- speaker (when using direct speech).

Activity 4

Using all the work you have done so far, write your response to the following task:

Your favourite magazine is running a creative writing competition. Write an imaginative short story suggested by the picture below.

Stage 3: Proofreading

Activity 5

a When you have finished your short story, you need to proofread your work. Check for accuracy in your writing, including:

- paragraphing
- a range of different sentence types
- spelling (use a dictionary where needed)
- capital letters for proper nouns, the beginning of sentences and the start of direct speech.

Beware of including too much direct speech. Some conversation is fine, but it should not make up the majority of your story.

Read your work aloud to check that it all makes sense and is punctuated correctly. Make any changes to improve your work.

b Read your first paragraph to your partner. Will it 'hook' your reader? Make any changes needed.

4 The collecting bug

Skills and objectives

- To examine how a writer uses whole text structure and sentence forms to achieve effects **(AO2)**

- To select and synthesize evidence from different texts **(AO1)**

- To compare writers' ideas and perspectives **(AO3)**

Writers shape and structure their ideas in order to help the reader understand their meaning. They do this by considering two things:

- whole text structure
- sentence forms.

Whole text structure

A successful piece of writing is like a journey. Your route is controlled by the writer. The writer controls what you see, for how long and where you go. There is a beginning, a middle and a final destination.

In the newspaper article on page 31, the writer's argument follows a logical sequence to show the reader that some people think collecting cockroaches can be fun. He weaves in other points that show most people take the opposite point of view.

Activity 1

a The writer has used eight paragraphs in the article. Rearrange the following paragraph summaries into the correct sequence from 1–8.

A Darren's interest started because of a gift of four cockroaches from his teacher.

B An environmental health officer believes cockroaches are a health hazard.

C Darren is about to travel abroad to study other cockroaches.

D Most people dislike cockroaches because they think they are dirty and spread disease.

E Cockroaches are great survivors and are difficult to exterminate.

F Darren's family are happy with his hobby.

G Cockroaches are actually clean insects and Darren thinks people dislike them just because of their lifestyle.

H Darren likes cockroaches and looks after 2000 of them.

b How does the opening paragraph engage the reader?

c Identify which paragraphs are not about Darren. Why do you think the writer has included some paragraphs about Darren and others about another topic?

d Explain how the final paragraph is a neat conclusion to the article. Use short quotations to support your explanation.

'The creepy subject of Darren's collecting bug'

1 The day Darren Mann left primary school his teacher presented him with a parting gift – four hissing cockroaches. It was a wonderful present, he recalls. They make lovely pets.

2 It's very much a minority view. Few creepy crawlies have a poorer public image than the humble cockroach. Associated with poor hygiene and the spread of disease, it's a target for extermination wherever it raises its ugly head.

3 But it has a passionate defender in Darren Mann. He keeps about two thousand of the little beasts in a garden shed at the family home, where he spends hours every day feeding them sliced apple and specialist food prepared for pet rats. He likes nothing better than to put his hand into a squirming tankful and let them tickle his fingers.

4 The very thought makes environmental health officer[1] George Makin cringe. He says that the common cockroach is rapidly moving up the public enemy list. He has recently had to close down several food premises and has no hesitation in describing the cockroach as a health hazard, a carrier of diseases like salmonella that must be rooted out and eradicated[2] wherever it is found.

5 That's by no means easy. Cockroaches are among the great survivors of the animal kingdom. They'll eat almost anything, including each other and the paste used to stick on wallpaper, and they can live in the tiniest crack in the skirting board.

6 Darren believes cockroaches are being unfairly maligned[3]. He's not convinced they are a major cause of the spread of salmonella and he says that it's their lifestyle, scuttling far and wide in search of food under cover of darkness, that makes them unloved. Despite the dirty brown appearance of the British cockroach, all cockroaches actually spend almost half their waking moments cleaning themselves, he reveals.

7 Darren's parents are quite happy about several thousand cockroaches living at the bottom of the garden. And Darren's girlfriend takes it in her stride too. 'She thinks they're quite cute actually,' he says, 'although she tends to scratch a bit when she comes out of the shed.'

8 As an insect collector who can't pass a stone without lifting it to see what's underneath, Darren is about to broaden his horizons. Next month he's off to Madagascar with a party of fellow enthusiasts to study some of the more exotic species of cockroach in their natural habitat. He's itching to get there.

[1]environmental health officer – a person whose job is to check
[2]eradicated – destroyed that the places where people live and work are safe and healthy
[3]maligned – spoken about critically

Writing can be shaped in many different ways. One text structure that we can see in this article is to begin with something small and zoom out to something much bigger: this starts 'in a garden shed' and ends with Darren 'off to Madagascar'. This is a bit like what we see all the time in films, with a close up or a long shot.

The text also shifts between a narrow focus on Darren who, for example, 'spends hours every day feeding them', and wider general information, such as 'Cockroaches are among the great survivors of the animal kingdom'. This positions Darren's life and interests in a wider context of society and the whole world.

Activity 2

Which of the following text structures also apply to the article on page 31?

a Zooming in from something big to something much smaller

b Shifting between different times

c A gradual introduction of new characters at significant points

d Moving from inside to the wider outside world

e Following a circular shape to shift focus through a series of points and end up back at the beginning

f Combining external actions with internal thoughts

g Shifting between different points of view

h Moving from the wider outside world to inside

i Shifting between different places

j Developing and repeating: focusing on a main point of view by expanding and repeating it

Sentence forms

A successful piece of writing often uses a variety of sentence forms. Different types of sentences can be used to create different effects. You should choose sentence types carefully in your own writing.

There are four main types of sentences:

● A **simple sentence** is made up of a single clause. It has a subject and one main verb. For example:

'They make lovely pets.'

subject   verb

● A **compound sentence** is made up of two or more simple sentences joined together. For example,

'They'll eat almost anything and they can live in the tiniest crack in the skirting board.

This could stand alone as a simple sentence.

This is a conjunction that links the two clauses together.

This could also stand alone as a simple sentence.

● A **complex sentence** has a main clause (which could stand alone as a simple sentence) and a dependent clause (which could not stand alone as a sentence). For example:

'The day Darren Mann left primary school his teacher presented him with a parting gift.'

This clause cannot stand alone. It is dependent on the main clause.

This is the main clause. It could stand alone as a sentence.

● A **minor sentence** is a short sentence consisting of very few words used deliberately to create an effect. For example, 'four hissing cockroaches!'

Activity 3

a In small groups, look at the sentences below and match them to possible effects that they create. Add the correct term to define the sentence type being used.

Sentences

A But it has a passionate defender in Darren Mann.

B They'll eat almost anything and they can live in the tiniest crack in the skirting board.

C The day Darren Mann left primary school his teacher presented him with a parting gift.

Possible effects

i This _____ sentence sets up a contrast between popular views and Mann's view.

ii This _____ sentence adds humour to the article. The reader is puzzled and wants to read on to find out why.

iii This _____ sentence adds detailed information that the reader needs to help them understand the situation.

b Now work with a partner to select another sentence from the article on page 31. Explain its effect in the article. Use the examples above to help you explain your sentence.

You are now going to use all the work you have done so far on both whole text structure and sentence forms.

Activity 4

a Read the student response to the example question below. There is no evidence to support the good points made.

b Find four places where quotations could strengthen the points made. Then choose relevant quotations to insert to raise this student's grade.

> Question: How has the writer structured the article to engage the reader?

In the article about Darren Mann, the writer uses whole text structure to organize the story and inform the reader about his unusual hobby. In the introduction the writer gives information about how Mann's hobby started. He alternates between close focus on Mann with a wider focus on what most other people think about cockroaches. The structure of the article is neat with circular structure – it begins and ends with Darren Mann and his hobby.

The writer also uses different sentence structures to give information and important points to interest the reader. For example he uses a simple sentence to emphasize Mann's love of cockroaches which is unusual and funny. He uses compound sentences to build up general facts and information about cockroaches to inform the reader.

Darren Mann started his cockroach collection in the 1980s, but collecting insects first became popular back in the 19th century.

In the extract on page 35, Charles Darwin, a famous naturalist, recalls how much he enjoyed this hobby while at university.

Extract from *Autobiography of Charles Darwin* by Charles Darwin, 1887

No pursuit at Cambridge was followed with nearly so much eagerness or gave me so much pleasure as collecting beetles. It was the mere passion for collecting, for I did not dissect[1] them, and rarely compared their external characters with published descriptions, but got them named anyhow. I will
5 give a proof of my zeal[2]: one day, on tearing off some old bark, I saw two rare beetles, and seized one in each hand; then I saw a third and new kind, which I could not bear to lose, so that I popped the one which I held in my right hand into my mouth. Alas! It ejected[3] some intensely acrid[4] fluid, which burnt my tongue so that I was forced to spit the beetle out, which was lost, as was
10 the third one.

I was very successful in collecting and inventing two new methods; I employed a labourer to scrape, during the winter, moss off old trees and place it in a large bag, and likewise to collect the rubbish at the bottom of the barges in which reeds are brought from the fens[5], and thus I got some
15 very rare species. No poet ever felt more delighted at seeing his first poem published than I did at seeing, in Stephen's 'Illustrations of British Insects', the magic words "captured by C. Darwin, Esq."

[1]dissect – cut up, to study something in parts
[2]zeal – enthusiasm
[3]ejected – spurted out
[4]acrid – bitter
[5]fens – flat lands in eastern England

Key term 🔑

Synthesize: to combine information and ideas from different texts

The newspaper article about Darren Mann and the extract from Charles Darwin's autobiography both deal with the subject of collecting bugs, but they are written in different centuries and from different perspectives. You are going to select and **synthesize** evidence from the two texts.

Activity (5)

a Work with a partner. Read through the extract again and see if you can summarize what Darwin reveals. Your challenge is to use only three clear sentences to structure your summary.

b Join with another pair to share your summaries. Check that you have not missed any key information.

Activity 6

a Discuss the similarities and differences between the descriptions of collecting insects in the two extracts on pages 31 and 35. Fill in a table like the one below to plan your comparison. The first row has been done for you.

Point of comparison	'The creepy subject of Darren's collecting bug'	Autobiography of Charles Darwin
Each collector's attitude to their hobby	He regards his cockroaches as pets.	He collects them to name them and to try to find rare species.
How involved each collector is		
The lengths they go to for their hobby		
Others' involvement in their hobby		

Activity 7

Using both texts and the plan you completed in Activity 6, write your response to the following question:

> Write a summary of the differences and similarities between Darwin's and Mann's interest in collecting bugs. Use your own words but also quote from both texts to support what you say.

Writing tip

When you compare two texts, use one paragraph for each point of comparison. Write about both texts in that paragraph so that you really are combining information about two pieces of writing. Analyse whether they are similar or different in terms of that point of comparison.

Progress check

In this chapter you have developed some key skills. Complete the progress check below to see how confident you now feel about applying these skills.

Key skills	Confident I understand how to do this.	OK Sometimes I understand how to do this.	Not sure I need to practise this more.
I can identify and interpret information and ideas.			
I can select and summarize evidence from the text(s) to support my views.			
I can analyse how the writer uses rhetorical questions and emotive language.			
I can understand how the writer uses whole text structure and sentence forms to achieve effects.			
I can compare writers' ideas and perspectives.			
I can communicate imaginatively, creating character and atmosphere in narrative writing.			
I can organize my ideas so that my writing is clear and accurate.			
I can use a variety of sentence forms.			

Assessment

This section tests all the reading and writing skills that you have learned in this chapter to see if you are able to apply them to different sources.

Read the article below and then complete the activities that follow.

A bug's life: Bed bugs are back and living under a mattress near you!

THOUSANDS of families across the land are engaged in all-out war. The enemy? That remarkably hardy little beast, the bed bug.

by Rachel Carlyle

1. A fact of life in Victorian Britain but thought almost extinct by the 1980s, this unwelcome guest is making an alarming comeback. Pest control company Rentokil reports a 70% increase in cases in the past three years, and the epidemic[1] shows no sign of abating.

2. Bed bugs are small, rust-coloured creatures about the size of an apple pip. They can't fly, or even crawl very fast, but they are incredible survivors. During the day they live in crevices – the wooden frame of your bed or bedside table is ideal. Then at night they crawl out to feed off your blood. They can be difficult to detect because more than half of us don't react to the first bite. Another 10 per cent never react at all. Many people take weeks or even months to notice, and by then they have an infestation[2] on their hands.

3. Company director Torie Chilcott knows exactly what that feels like. She and her family, from East Molesey in Surrey, had trouble with bugs following a trip to the Philippines. They assumed the problem had been solved after a mammoth spring-clean and chemical-spraying session, but when Torie's nine-year-old son Archie arrived at her bedroom doorway one morning covered in bites, she searched his bed and immediately found the culprits[3].

4. 'There were loads of them – on the bedding, hidden in the bed frame and even on his teddies. It was absolutely disgusting,' she says. 'I took two days off work and stripped the place. All the bedding went, the curtains went to the cleaners – I was like a woman possessed.' Torie also called in a pest-control team who sprayed chemicals all over the room. 'The bugs never got as far as my daughter Kate's bedroom,' she says. 'We were told they probably couldn't be bothered to go any further because they had everything they wanted in Archie's room – him.'

5. Contrary to popular opinion, bed bugs are not the result of poor domestic hygiene. If you have them, they probably hitched a lift in your luggage during your last holiday abroad. Hotels are a big source, as are cruise ships, hostels and even airline seats. Pest controllers told Torie Chilcott that her son's bugs had probably migrated from suitcases stored in a cupboard next to his room.

6. The bugs' resurgence[4] since the 1980s may be because they are developing immunity[5] to certain poisons, or it may simply reflect a more mobile human population. Either way, David Cain of London-based pest controllers Bed Bugs Ltd puts the problem in stark terms: 'I've heard it said that once you have stayed in 20 hotels, theoretically you will have picked them up.'

[1]epidemic – a quickly spreading disease
[2]infestation – a troublesome number of pests
[3]culprits – guilty people or creatures
[4]resurgence – increase
[5]immunity – resistance

This activity will secure your knowledge about **how to identify and interpret information (AO1)**.

Activity 1

a Look at the first paragraph of the article on page 38. Find *four* true statements about bed bugs in this paragraph.

b Now look at the second paragraph. This contains both explicit and implicit ideas. Write *one* sentence that summarizes what is implied about bed bugs.

This activity will secure your knowledge about **how writers use text structure and sentence forms to create effects (AO2)**.

Activity 2

a Read the structural features listed below and link them to the relevant paragraph(s).

- Conclusion
- Moving from inside to the wider outside world
- Life story/real-life example
- Introduction
- Factual information about bed bugs

b Identify the types of sentences used by the writer below and explain their effect on the reader. The table below might help you to plan your answer.

Sentence	Sentence type	Explanation of effect
'Then at night they crawl out to feed on your blood.'	Complex sentence	The writer uses a main clause to explain what the bed bugs do, and a subordinate clause to explain why.
'They can't fly, or even crawl very fast, but they are incredible survivors.'		
'It was absolutely disgusting.'		

This activity will remind you **how writers use language to create effects for the reader (AO2)**.

Activity 3

a The writer uses the words 'epidemic' in the first paragraph and 'infestation' in the second paragraph. What does her choice of language tell us about bed bugs?

b In the sentence 'Then at night they crawl out to feed off your blood', what effect do the words 'crawl' and 'feed' have on the reader?

Now read the following extract from a book about medical practices, written in 1837. Leeches were popularly used to suck people's blood at this time for medical reasons. It was thought that releasing human blood would make sick people better.

Men and women collected leeches as their job. Leech collectors would wade in leech-infested waters, allowing the leeches to attach themselves to the collectors' legs. Leeches were in high demand at this time and some countries had to import them to have enough for human use.

Extract from *Curiosities of Medical Experience* by J. G. Millignen

If ever you pass through La Brenne, you will see a man, pale and straight-haired, with a woollen cap on his head, and his legs and arms naked; he walks along the borders of a marsh, among the spots left
5 dry by the surrounding waters. This man is a leech-fisher. To see him from a distance,—his woebegone[1] aspect, his hollow eyes, his livid lips, his singular gestures, you would take him for a maniac. If you observe him every now and then raising his legs
10 and examining them one after another, you might suppose him a fool; but he is an intelligent leech-fisher. The leeches attach themselves to his legs and feet as he moves among their haunts[2]; he feels their bite, and gathers them as they cluster about
15 the roots of the bulrushes and aquatic weeds, or beneath the stones covered with a green and slimy moss. He may thus collect ten or twelve dozen in three or four hours. In summer, when the leeches retire into deep water, the fishers move about upon
20 rafts made of twigs and rushes. One of these traders was known to collect, with the aid of his children, seventeen thousand five hundred leeches in the course of a few months; these he had deposited in a reservoir, where, in one night, they were all frozen
25 *en masse*. But congelation[3] does not kill them, and they can easily be thawed into life, by melting the ice that surrounds them. Leeches, it appears, can bear much rougher usage than one might imagine: they are packed up closely in wet bags, carried on pack-
30 saddles, and it is well known that they will attach themselves with more avidity[4] when rubbed in a dry napkin previous to their application. [...]

Leeches kept in a glass bottle may serve as a barometer[5], as they invariably ascend or descend in the water as the weather changes from dry to 35 wet, and they generally rise to the surface prior to a thunder-storm. They are most voracious[6], and are frequently observed to destroy one another by suction; the strong ones attaching themselves to the weaker. 40

The quantity of blood drawn by leeches has been a subject of much controversy[7]; but it is pretty nearly ascertained[8] that a healthy leech, when fully gorged, has extracted about half an ounce. [...]

Norfolk supplies the greater part of the leeches 45 brought to London, but they are also found in Kent, Suffolk, Essex, and Wales. The leeches imported from France differ from ours, in having the belly of one uniform colour. The best are the green, with yellow stripes along the body. The horse-leech, which 50 is used in the north of Europe, but also common in England, is entirely brown, or only marked with a marginal yellow line. A popular belief prevails, that the application of this variety is most dangerous, as they are said to suck out all the blood in the body. 55

[1]woebegone – miserable
[2]haunts – places often visited
[3]congelation – the process of becoming or the state of being congealed i.e. becoming solid instead of a liquid, or frozen
[4]avidity – enthusiasm
[5]barometer – a device that predicts the weather
[6]voracious – greedy
[7]controversy – debate
[8]ascertained – confirmed

Both extracts on pages 38 and 40 deal with bugs and their relationship with humans, but they were written in different centuries and from different perspectives. You are going to find and combine evidence from both texts to consider their similarities and differences. Then you will go on to start comparing the texts.

This activity will secure your knowledge about **how to compare writers' points of view about their chosen topic (AO3)**. You will also **select and synthesize evidence from different texts (AO1)**.

Activity 4

a Use the table below to compare the information given about the creatures in each article and their relationship with humans.

	Bed bugs	Leeches
Similarities between the bugs		
Differences between the bugs		
Similarities in their relationship with humans		
Differences in their relationship with humans		

b Decide whether the writer of each article has a positive, negative or mixed point of view about the bug they are writing about. Complete the sentences below:

- I think the writer of the article about leeches has a positive/negative/mixed view about leeches. This is because…

- I think the writer of the article about bed bugs has a positive/negative/mixed view about bed bugs. This is because…

Activity 5

Using your answers to Activity 4 on page 41 as well as any other similarities or differences in the two texts, write a two-paragraph response to the following task:

> Write a summary of the similarities and differences between bed bugs today and leeches in the nineteenth century and the writers' views on them. Use your own words but also quote from both texts to support what you say.

You might like to use some of the sentence starters below to structure your writing:

- Both leeches and bed bugs are…
- They are different because…
- They are similar because…
- Both have a close relationship with humans…
- The writers have different perspectives on the bugs they write about. For example,…

This activity will secure your knowledge of **how to evaluate writing using references to the text (AO4)**. Note that in the exam this question will relate to a fiction text, but the same skills can be applied to both fiction and non-fiction texts.

Activity 6

a Look back at the two information texts on bed bugs (page 38) and leeches (page 40). Decide which one you think is most successful at being informative and interesting for the reader. Remember to think carefully about the effects that the writer has created using language and structure.

b Explain which text is the 'winner' for you and choose two quotations from that text as evidence for your opinion.

This activity will secure your knowledge of **how to write an imaginative story, using clear, accurate English (AO5, AO6)**.

Activity 7

Write a short narrative story suggested by the photograph below.

Remember to:

- plan the plot (what happens)
- think about characters – their appearance and personality
- use language to create a particular atmosphere
- make your opening interest the reader
- organize your writing in paragraphs
- proofread your work, checking spelling, punctuation and grammar.

2 Fight for freedom

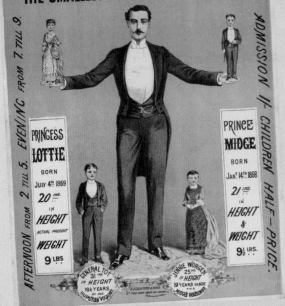

PICCADILLY HALL.
HARVEY'S MIDGES
THE SMALLEST PEOPLE IN THE WORLD.

AFTERNOON FROM 2 TILL 5. EVENING FROM 7 TILL 9.

ADMISSION 1/- CHILDREN HALF-PRICE.

PRINCESS
LOTTIE
BORN
JULY 4TH 1869
20 INS.
IN
HEIGHT
ACTUAL PRESENT
WEIGHT
9 LBS

PRINCE
MIDGE
BORN
JANY 14TH 1868
21 INS
IN
HEIGHT
&
WEIGHT
9½ LBS.

'Freedom!' is the cry which has echoed throughout history, across continents as people have risen up against those in power. It is a cry of protest, but also of hope that things can change.

In this chapter, you will hear the voices of people fighting for their freedom – freedom from prejudice (unfair dislike or judgement) and from oppression (unfair treatment or rule by the powerful).
For many of them, writing about their experiences is the only way they can express how they feel and communicate with the wider world.

Activity

a Discuss the four images on pages 44–45 with a partner. They each show a historical event or attitude.

- What events, people or prejudices do they show?
- Which one do you find most upsetting and why?

b Which current news stories can you think of that relate to prejudice and oppression? (Scan the week's news stories to help you.) In small groups make a list of recent news stories linked to this topic. You might consider issues around the world, relating to:

- race or immigration
- war
- equality between men and women
- politics and power
- poverty and social class
- money and power
- disability.

Skills and Assessment Objectives

All the reading and writing skills in this chapter are linked to the Assessment Objectives (AOs) for GCSE English Language.

Reading skills include how to:

- identify and interpret ideas
- find and use quotations
- combine information from different texts
- explore the effects of language and structure
- compare and evaluate texts.

Writing skills include how to:

- write in different ways for different people
- adapt your writing to match your audience
- write effectively and imaginatively
- organize ideas clearly.

1 Written in black and white

- To identify and interpret explicit and implicit ideas **(AO1)**

- To select evidence from texts **(AO1)**

- To comment on and analyse language **(AO2)**

- To compare writers' ideas and how they are conveyed **(AO3)**

Key term 🔑

Explicit: clearly stated; you just need to find it

In 1963, Martin Luther King gave a speech against racial prejudice at a demonstration in Washington, USA. He was speaking at a time when there was extreme discrimination against non-white people in America. Read the extract, looking out for **explicit** points that King makes.

Extract from a transcript of a speech by Martin Luther King

I am happy to join with you today in what will go down in history as the greatest demonstration for freedom in the history of our nation. [...] There are those who are asking the devotees of civil rights[1]: 'When will you be satisfied?' We can never be satisfied as long as the Negro[2] is the victim of
5 the unspeakable horrors of police brutality. We can never be satisfied as long as our bodies, heavy with the fatigue of travel, cannot gain lodging in the motels of the highways and the hotels of the cities. We cannot be satisfied as long as the Negro's basic mobility is from a smaller ghetto to a larger one. We can never be satisfied as long as our children are stripped of
10 their selfhood and robbed of their dignity by signs stating 'For Whites Only'. We cannot be satisfied and we will not be satisfied as long as a Negro in Mississippi cannot vote and a Negro in New York believes he has nothing for which to vote. No, no, we are not satisfied, and we will not be satisfied until 'justice rolls down like waters and righteousness like a mighty stream'.

[1]civil rights – the rights of people to have equality, freedom to speak and a right to vote
[2]'Negro' – a term that is considered offensive nowadays and should be avoided, but it wasn't at the time when this speech was delivered

---

Activity ①

Look at the table below. For each explicit idea listed, select a quotation from the extract above to support it.

Explicit idea	Selected quotation
The police are unfair in their treatment of black people.	'the Negro is the victim of the unspeakable horrors of police brutality'
Some hotels do not allow black people to stay there.	
Children are treated differently depending on the colour of their skin.	
Black people in Mississippi do not have the right to vote.	

When writing about texts, you need to provide evidence to support each point you make. This evidence should be a quotation from the text. A quotation can be a sentence, phrase or a single word. Keep quotations short; choose a word or phrase rather than long chunks of text.

You can include quotations in three ways:

1. Introduced by a phrase such as 'for example', 'he says…' or 'this is shown by the phrase'.

In his speech, King is protesting against racism. He says 'we will not be satisfied as long as a Black person in Mississippi cannot vote'.

2. A colon after your point, followed by the quotation.

In his speech, King is protesting against racism: 'we will not be satisfied as long as a Black person in Mississippi cannot vote'.

3. Woven into the same sentence as the point you are making.

In his speech, King is protesting against racism, as he writes 'we will not be satisfied as long as a Black person in Mississippi cannot vote'.

> **Tips** ✓
>
> - Always refer to the writer by their last name, for example, King or Dickens, not Martin or Charles!
>
> - Write your explanation in the present tense. The speech still exists even though it was made in the past.

Activity 2

a Share the quotations in your table from Activity 1 with a partner. Discuss where you could use shorter quotations and whether they would still make sense as examples.

b Write up the explicit ideas from your table as a single paragraph. Use the quotations you have chosen to support the ideas you have identified. Use the sentence below to begin your explanation:

> In his speech, King makes a number of key points…

King hopes that things will change in America. The phrase 'rise up' suggests that he hopes there will be a surge of energy against the way things are now.

King believes that…

King hopes that…

King speaks of his dream that…

King's strong hope is that…

Extract from a transcript of a speech by Martin Luther King

I have a dream that one day this nation will rise up and live out the true meaning of its creed[1]: we hold these truths to be self-evident: that all men are created equal.

5 I have a dream that one day on the red hills of Georgia the sons of former slaves and the sons of former slave-owners will be able to sit down together at a table of brotherhood.

I have a dream that one day even the state of Mississippi, a desert state, sweltering with the heat of injustice and oppression, will be transformed into
10 an oasis[2] of freedom and justice.

I have a dream that my four little children will one day live in a nation where they will not be judged by the colour of their skin but by the content of their character.

I have a dream today!

[1]creed – beliefs
[2]oasis – a fertile place in a desert

Activity 3

Read the above extract from the speech. What do you understand from this extract about Martin Luther King's hopes for the future?

- Look carefully at the highlighted sections to work out what King's words imply about his hopes and beliefs. An example and sentence starters have been done for you.

- Write a paragraph about King's hopes and beliefs. Remember to use quotations to support your points. Use the sentence starter below to begin your paragraph.

In this section of the speech, King conveys his hopes for the future. He…

Key terms

Implicit: suggested; you have to **interpret** the text to work it out for yourself

Interpret: explain the meaning of something in your own words, showing your understanding

To show a more developed understanding of the texts you read, you must explore their **implicit** meaning. This means explaining what is suggested or hinted at, rather than what is openly stated. For example:

In his speech, King is protesting against racism, as he writes 'we will not be satisfied as long as a Negro in Mississippi cannot vote'. The phrase 'not be satisfied' suggests his determination that life for black people must change.

This is the explicit (surface) idea.

This is the quotation.

This is an implicit meaning of the text.

King doesn't use the word 'determined' explicitly in the speech; it is something he implies and which the reader can work out.

King was a skilled speaker. His speech uses many rhetorical devices to convey his ideas powerfully.

To show your reading confidence you need to be able to identify the language and devices that skilled writers use. You should consider what their effect is on the reader or audience.

Activity 4

Look again at the extract from Martin Luther King's speech on page 48.

a King uses *pairs of opposites* to emphasize how things can change. Find the opposite of the four ideas below that add balance to King's speech:

- slaves
- desert
- heat of oppression
- colour of their skin

b He uses *repetition* to add rhythm and emphasis to his speech. Which key phrase is repeated? How many times is it used?

The black poet Benjamin Zephaniah is famous for making a stand against the prejudice that many black people have endured – and still do. He wrote the following article after he was told that the Queen wanted to give him an official honour – an OBE (Order of the British Empire).

Extract from *The Guardian*, 27 November 2003

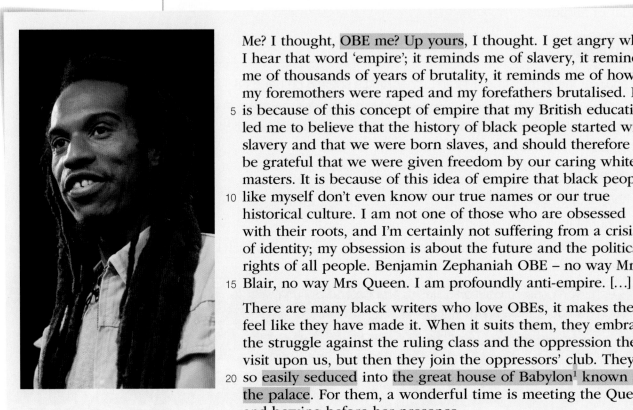

Me? I thought, OBE me? Up yours, I thought. I get angry when I hear that word 'empire'; it reminds me of slavery, it reminds me of thousands of years of brutality, it reminds me of how my foremothers were raped and my forefathers brutalised. It
5 is because of this concept of empire that my British education led me to believe that the history of black people started with slavery and that we were born slaves, and should therefore be grateful that we were given freedom by our caring white masters. It is because of this idea of empire that black people
10 like myself don't even know our true names or our true historical culture. I am not one of those who are obsessed with their roots, and I'm certainly not suffering from a crisis of identity; my obsession is about the future and the political rights of all people. Benjamin Zephaniah OBE – no way Mr
15 Blair, no way Mrs Queen. I am profoundly anti-empire. […]

There are many black writers who love OBEs, it makes them feel like they have made it. When it suits them, they embrace the struggle against the ruling class and the oppression they visit upon us, but then they join the oppressors' club. They are
20 so easily seduced into the great house of Babylon[1] known as the palace. For them, a wonderful time is meeting the Queen and bowing before her presence.

I was shocked to see how many of my fellow writers jumped at the opportunity to go to Buckingham Palace when the
25 Queen had her 'meet the writers day' on July 9 2002, and I laughed at the pathetic excuses writers gave for going. 'I did it for my mum'; 'I did it for my kids'; 'I did it for the school'; 'I did it for the people', etc. I have even heard black writers who have collected OBEs saying that it is 'symbolic of how far we
30 have come'. Oh yes, I say, we've struggled so hard just to get a minute with the Queen and we are so very grateful – not.

[1]Babylon – Babylon is an ancient city in what is now called Iraq. In Zephaniah's religion, Rastafari, it links to the capitalist world where materialism and luxury are valued above all other things. In the Bible it stands for a place of sin.

Activity 5

Key term

Adjective: a word that describes something named by a noun or pronoun

a Re-read the first paragraph.

SPAG

i Choose three **adjectives** from the list below which you think best describe how Zephaniah feels about being offered the OBE. Use a dictionary if you need to.

insulted   delighted   embarrassed

disappointed   surprised   angry

worried   contemptuous   excited

ii Select a quotation to support each choice.

b Now re-read the rest of the article where Zephaniah expresses disgust at other black writers that accept OBEs. Think about how he uses language to convey his disgust; match the comments below to the correct highlighted quotations from Zephaniah's article. One example is done for you.

i Zephaniah uses critical adjectives to emphasize his negative feelings about writers who accept OBEs and their actions. For example, he uses the word 'pathetic'.

ii Zephaniah uses slang to emphasize his difference from the Queen and the British establishment. For example...

iii Zephaniah uses sarcasm to emphasize that he is different from other writers who accept OBEs. For example...

iv Zephaniah uses direct quotations to mock other writers who make excuses for accepting OBEs. For example...

v Zephaniah uses verbs that are associated with love to mock the writers whose actions suggest they admire the Queen and what she represents. For example...

vi Zephaniah uses Biblical references to suggest that the palace is an institution linked with past sins. For example...

Now you are going to compare the *way* Martin Luther King and Benjamin Zephaniah convey their strong views about the white powerful rulers to their intended audiences.

Look back at the extracts from King's speech (page 46 and 48) and Zephaniah's article (page 50).

Key term

Figurative language: imaginative language that is used to convey an idea. It can use a comparison or a sound, for interest, or to illustrate an idea rather than stating it explicitly. Examples include simile, metaphor, personification and alliteration

Activity 6

a Look back at the extracts from King's speech (page 46 and 48) and Zephaniah's article (page 50). With a partner, discuss and agree which of the following features are displayed in one or both texts.

Feature	King's speech	Zephaniah's article
Formal language		
Informal language		
Pairs of opposites		
Repetition		
Powerful verbs		
Adjectives for particular effects (e.g. to create a visual picture, to criticize)		
Familiar references (e.g. the Bible)		
Quotations/proof from real-life experience		
Use of the first person plural 'we'		
Sarcasm		
Figurative language		

b Select two of the features above and explain their effect in the protest against white authority. Use the Point, Evidence, Explanation (PEE) structure. An example has been done for you:

> Both texts use the first person 'we'. For example King says 'we can never be satisfied'. Zephaniah writes that he wrongly believed 'we were born slaves'. Both men use this to show they feel linked to all other black people and separate from the established power of society.

Point

Evidence

Explanation

c Look back at your writing comparing the two texts. Consider the connectives below that work well to structure comparative writing texts:

comparing **similarly** **in the same way** **in contrast**

however **on the other hand** **whereas**

i How many of these have you used already?

ii Can you identify any places where these could be inserted to improve your writing?

Marchers in Union Station, Washington D.C.

2 Speaking out

Skills and objectives

- To organize information in order to communicate clearly and effectively **(AO5)**
- To check the clarity and accuracy of your work **(AO6)**

There are many different forms of prejudice in our society. People can be victims of prejudice on the grounds of race, colour, religion, gender, sexuality, age, appearance or disability.

In this section, you will be writing an article about prejudice, but first look at the extract below to remind yourself of some key features of news articles. This extract is the opening of an article highlighting the prejudice against gay footballers.

Extract from an article on Stonewall website, 2009

FA and Premier League slammed by fans for failure to tackle anti-gay abuse

The Football Association faces calls for immediate action as authoritative[1] research demonstrates that anti-gay abuse in the sport has been witnessed by seven in ten fans. The new Stonewall[2] research also reveals that fans now expect visible action from the FA.

5 'Leagues behind – Football's failure to tackle anti-gay abuse' features a YouGov survey of over 2,000 football fans from across Britain and interviews with top football insiders and lesbian and gay players. It finds that:
- Three in five fans believe anti-gay abuse from fans dissuades gay players from coming out
10 - Almost two thirds of fans believe football would be a better sport if anti-gay abuse was eradicated
- Two thirds of fans would feel comfortable if a player on their team came out
- Over half of fans think the FA, Premier League and Football League are not doing enough to tackle anti-gay abuse.

15 'Sadly, this survey demonstrates that football is institutionally homophobic[3]', says Ben Summerskill, Stonewall's Chief Executive. 'Too little action has been taken about an issue which deters not just gay players and fans from enjoying our national game, but also thousands of other fans too. Football has a firm track record tackling problems 20 such as hooliganism and racism. But anti-gay abuse still almost always goes unchallenged. When England is looking to host and win the 2018 World Cup, football 25 cannot risk this loss of potential talent and supporters.'

[1]authoritative – expert or official
[2]Stonewall – an organization that campaigns for equality and justice for lesbian, gay and bisexual people
[3]homophobic – having an irrational dislike and fear of gay people

Activity 1

a With a partner, decide how you would complete the statement below to show your understanding of the article.

As a result of research from the organization _____ , the FA understand that they have to _____ homophobic attitudes in football. Both _____ and _____ believe that the FA are not _____ about homophobia in the sport.

b Identify two *statistics* (information given as numbers) that are used as evidence in this text.

c Identify two *named specialist organizations* or *people* that are used as evidence in this information text.

d List any *specialist vocabulary* about the topic of football that is used to show the journalist's knowledge about this topic.

e Which of the following features are used by the writer to structure this extract: introduction, subheadings, lists, headline, interviews, bullet points?

Writing tip

When writing an article, remember to include:

- a headline
- an introduction
- separate paragraphs
- facts
- statistics
- names of people and places
- quotations.

Activity 2

Look at the images below. Which do you think would be most likely to be used in a newspaper article about today's teenagers?

Write an article about prejudice against teenagers in our society, as portrayed in the British media (newspapers, TV, magazines and websites). The headline of the article should be:

British media slammed for negative attitudes to today's teenagers

The purpose of the article is to inform, so your writing needs to contain relevant facts and opinions from real life. (You might decide to make up a few believable numbers, facts and quotations from specialists to combine with what you know about this topic.)

Use the stages on page 57–59 to help you plan, write and proofread your article.

Stage 1: Ideas and planning

1. Complete the first column of a table like the one below, listing the negative perceptions that the British media may promote about today's young people. Think about how teenagers are portrayed in the news, on programmes that you watch and by politicians. Some ideas have been noted for you.

2. Complete the second column with positive activities today's young people are involved in. Try to think about well-known teenagers that you could use as examples, or people that you know from your own school or community.

3. Share your ideas with a partner and consider any extra ideas that they suggest.

Negative ideas portrayed by the media	Positive ideas that the media should consider
Sexting/teenage pregnancy/children growing up too fast	Famous teenagers, for example, Malala Yousafzai (who won the Nobel peace prize in 2014)
Materialism – children having smartphones, tablets and computer games	Charity work, for example, Duke of Edinburgh awards
…	…

4. Decide on two pictures to illustrate your article. They could be from this page or others that you have found. Give reasons for your choices.

5. Plan how you will structure your article. Decide which organizational devices you will use to present your ideas, such as headings, subheadings, paragraphs and bullet points. Use the template below to help you plan.

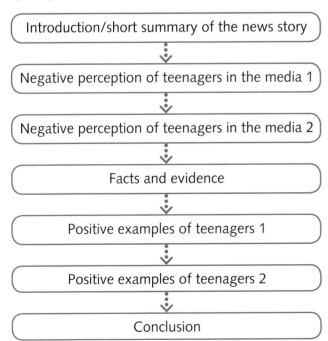

Introduction/short summary of the news story

↓

Negative perception of teenagers in the media 1

↓

Negative perception of teenagers in the media 2

↓

Facts and evidence

↓

Positive examples of teenagers 1

↓

Positive examples of teenagers 2

↓

Conclusion

Stage 2: Writing

- Look at the two student texts below. Read them aloud with a partner and identify their effect on the reader.

  - Which is more formal?

  - Which words and phrases would you need to change to improve the weaker example?

- Think carefully about the formal and impersonal style that you want to adopt in your own writing. Complete your article, using your plan to keep your writing on track.

Jayden

I don't think anyone should judge someone because of the way they look. It isn't right to think that kids wearing hoods are any more dangerous or uneducated than posh kids in a shirt and tie. Both groups can vandalize stuff; both groups might steal and groups can be lazy. On the other hand they can also both be ok. Many of my friends who might chill out on a Saturday in town are just the same guys that are working hard after school and doing well in their exams. It's not black and white.

George

While journalists have their right to their own opinions, they do not have the right to feed prejudice in society. Just in one week in January this year, 'The Daily Voice' ran 5 stories with negative ideas about teenagers. Particular examples include an old lady who was mugged by two teenagers, a disabled man whose life had become a misery because of taunts from young people and the death of a young person because of legal highs.

Stage 3: Proofreading

- Read your work again and check that you have kept a formal and impersonal style throughout.

- Proofread your work. Does it make sense? Are spellings and punctuation correct? Use a dictionary if you need to.

- Share your article with a partner. Invite them to suggest further changes to improve your work.

- Look at the **connectives** listed in the key term panel.

- Some connectives are used to indicate that one thing happens because of something else. Colour these connectives in red.

- Some connectives are used to extend a point by adding further information. Colour these connectives in blue.

- Can you add any connectives to improve your writing?

Key term

Connective: a word that joins phrases or sentences, such as *moreover, as a result, furthermore, in addition, not only… but also, because, therefore, consequently*

3 Big Brother

- To analyse how writers use language and structure to achieve effects **(AO2)**

- To evaluate texts critically, supporting with textual references **(AO4)**

In this section you will look at the opening of a famous novel, *Nineteen Eighty-Four.* The author George Orwell describes a fictional society where ruthless authorities silence anyone who disagrees with them. There is no freedom. Even people's thoughts are monitored.

Read the complete extract on page 61.

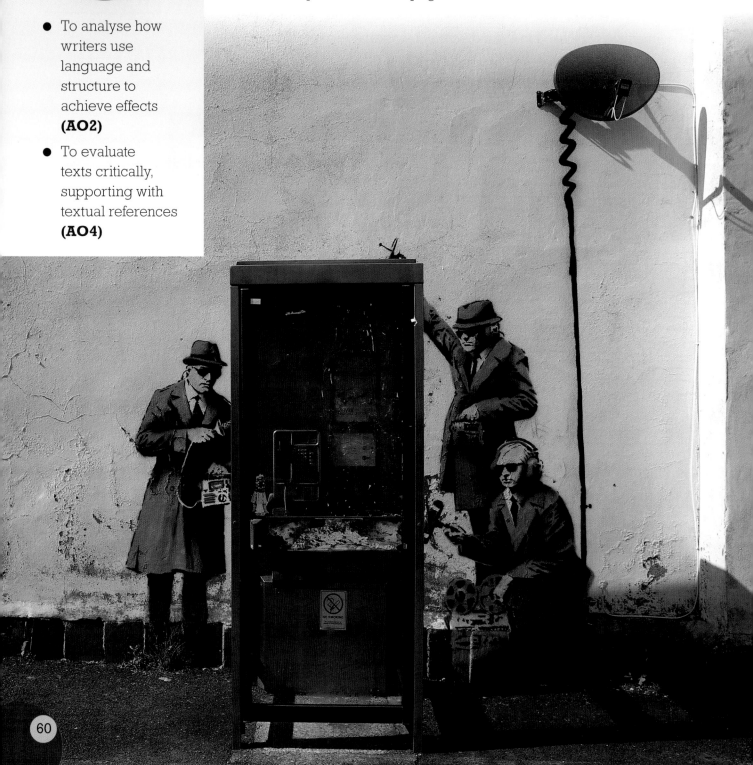

Extract from *Nineteen Eighty-Four* by George Orwell

It was a bright cold day in April, and the clocks were striking thirteen. Winston Smith, his chin nuzzled into his breast in an effort to escape the vile wind, slipped quickly through the glass doors of Victory Mansions, though not quickly enough to prevent a swirl of gritty dust from entering along with him.

5   The hallway smelt of boiled cabbage and old rag mats. At one end of it a coloured poster, too large for indoor display, had been tacked to the wall. It depicted simply an enormous face, more than a metre wide [...] Winston made for the stairs. It was no use trying the lift. Even at the best of times it was seldom working, and at present the electric current was cut off during daylight

10 hours. It was part of the economy drive in preparation for Hate Week. The flat was seven flights up [...] On each landing, opposite the lift-shaft, the poster with the enormous face gazed from the wall. It was one of those pictures which are so contrived that the eyes follow you about when you move. BIG BROTHER IS WATCHING YOU, the caption beneath it ran.

15 Inside the flat a fruity voice was reading out a list of figures which had something to do with the production of pig-iron. The voice came from an oblong metal plaque like a dulled mirror which formed part of the surface of the right-hand wall. Winston turned a switch and the voice sank somewhat, though the words were still distinguishable. The instrument (the telescreen,

20 it was called) could be dimmed, but there was no way of shutting it off completely. He moved over to the window: a smallish, frail figure, the meagreness of his body merely emphasized by the blue overalls which were the uniform of the party. His hair was very fair, his face naturally sanguine[1], his skin roughened by coarse[2] soap and blunt razor blades and the cold of the

25 winter that had just ended.

Outside, even through the shut window-pane, the world looked cold. Down in the street little eddies of wind were whirling dust and torn paper into spirals, and though the sun was shining and the sky a harsh blue, there seemed to

30 be no colour in anything, except the posters that were plastered everywhere. [...] In the far distance a helicopter skimmed down between the roofs, hovered for an instant like a bluebottle, and darted away again with a curving flight. It was the police patrol,

35 snooping into people's windows. The patrols did not matter, however. Only the Thought Police mattered.

[1]sanguine – hopeful and cheerful
[2]coarse – rough

Look carefully at how the structure of the text is built up in the extract on page 61. It is like a film, where the camera moves our view from one focus to another.

Opening sentence	First introductions	Setting the scene	Shifting focus	Spotlight on character	Wider perspectives

Opening sentence

Extract from *Nineteen Eighty-Four* by George Orwell

It was a bright cold day in April, and the clocks were striking thirteen.

The opening sentence in the structure of any text is very important because it needs to immediately interest the reader. It must have impact.

Activity 1

Orwell's first sentence appears to be very ordinary, but is it? Discuss the language of the sentence with a partner.

- Look carefully at the two **clauses** divided by 'and'.
- What is strange about the second clause?
- What effect does this have on the reader?

First introductions

Extract from *Nineteen Eighty-Four* by George Orwell

Winston Smith, his chin nuzzled into his breast in an effort to escape the vile wind, slipped quickly through the glass doors of Victory Mansions, though not quickly enough to prevent a swirl of gritty dust from entering along with him.

Having captured the reader's attention, the writer introduces a character, Winston, and where he lives. Structurally, Orwell uses a short paragraph to entice the reader to want to find out more.

Activity 2

a Look at the two proper nouns chosen by the writer to describe the main character and the place he lives in this extract. Draw two spider diagrams and note down the **connotations** of each word or phrase. These could be any particular feelings, ideas, images and memories that you associate with these names.

b Compare your ideas with a partner. How and why do they differ?

Winston Smith

Victory Mansions

Setting the scene

Extract from *Nineteen Eighty-Four* by George Orwell

The hallway smelt of boiled cabbage and old rag mats. At one end of it a coloured poster, too large for indoor display, had been tacked to the wall. It depicted simply an enormous face, more than a metre wide […] Winston made for the stairs. It was no use trying the lift. Even at the best of times it was seldom working, and at present the electric current was cut off during daylight hours. It was part of the economy drive in preparation for Hate Week. The flat was seven flights up […] On each landing, opposite the lift-shaft, the poster with the enormous face gazed from the wall. It was one of those pictures which are so contrived that the eyes follow you about when you move. BIG BROTHER IS WATCHING YOU, the caption beneath it ran.

The new paragraph indicates a change from the character to the **setting**.

Activity 3

With a partner, find any clues that suggest the society in which the character lives is unlike our own. Be prepared to explain your ideas with close reference to the text.

Shifting focus

Orwell uses a range of vocabulary in this extract. The words combine to create an overall impression of the place.

New focus. This sentence signals to the reader that action has moved inside, to add a closer view of the character's flat.

Extract from *Nineteen Eighty-Four* by George Orwell

Inside the flat a fruity voice was reading out a list of figures which had something to do with the production of pig-iron. The voice came from an oblong metal plaque like a dulled mirror which formed part of the surface of the right-hand wall. Winston turned a switch and the voice sank somewhat, though the words were still distinguishable. The instrument (the telescreen, it was called) could be dimmed, but there was no way of shutting it off completely.

Activity 4

a With a partner, read the words below. Decide which one summarizes the overall impression the writer is trying to create of this indoor setting. Use a dictionary to check on any words you are not sure of.

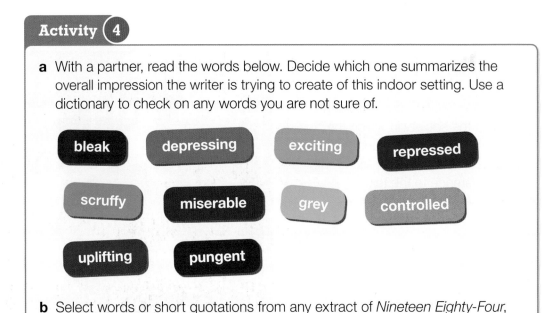

bleak   depressing   exciting   repressed

scruffy   miserable   grey   controlled

uplifting   pungent

b Select words or short quotations from any extract of *Nineteen Eighty-Four*, so far, which help build the impression you have chosen in Activity 4a.

Spotlight on character

Extract from *Nineteen Eighty-Four* by George Orwell

He moved over to the window: a smallish, frail figure, the meagreness of his body merely emphasized by the blue overalls which were the uniform of the party. His hair was very fair, his face naturally sanguine, his skin roughened by coarse soap and blunt razor blades and the cold of the winter that had just ended.

Now, like a film, the writer moves the camera focus on to Winston. The writer is using the text's structure to direct the reader towards the character.

Activity 5

a What does the word 'meagreness' suggest about Winston and his life?

b Why might he be wearing 'the uniform of the party'?

c What is the effect of describing his skin as 'roughened by coarse soap and blunt razor blades'?

Wider perspectives

Extract from *Nineteen Eighty-Four* by George Orwell

Outside, even through the shut window-pane, the world looked cold. Down in the street little eddies of wind were whirling dust and torn paper into spirals, and though the sun was shining and the sky a harsh blue, there seemed to be no colour in anything, except the posters that were plastered everywhere. [...] In the far distance a helicopter skimmed down between the roofs, hovered for an instant like a bluebottle, and darted away again with a curving flight. It was the police patrol, snooping into people's windows. The patrols did not matter, however. Only the Thought Police mattered.

Orwell uses the start of the paragraph to refocus the reader again. He uses the window like a camera viewfinder to widen the reader's perspective beyond the room.

Another reader has said, 'In this opening chapter the writer has created a bleak and oppressive (unfair and restricted) society that none of us would want to live in'.

a Look at the agreement line below. How far do you agree with the statement? Copy it and place your name next to the number that reflects your view.

Disagree ←——————————————→ Agree

1   2   3   4   5   6   7   8   9   10

b Now think about how the writer presents this society. With a partner, consider what we learn about:

- the natural world
- the political systems of the society
- the buildings inside and outside
- the people that live there.

c Write three PEE points that support your view on the timeline, using the bullet points above to help you. An example is listed for you, below.

The writer has presented quite a hostile society through his hints about the systems and politics. For example he mentions 'Thought Police' and the posters saying 'BIG BROTHER IS WATCHING YOU'. These all suggest that the people have no privacy and they are watched and checked all the time.

> Point

> Evidence

> Explanation

Progress check

In this chapter you have developed some key skills. Complete the progress check below to see how confident you now feel about applying these skills.

Key skills	Confident I understand how to do this.	OK Sometimes I understand how to do this.	Not sure I need to practise this more.
I can identify explicit and implicit ideas.			
I can select and summarize evidence.			
I can analyse the writer's use of language.			
I can analyse the writer's use of structure.			
I can compare writers' ideas.			
I can compare how writers convey their ideas.			
I can write an article to put forward a point of view.			
I can organize my ideas so my writing is well-structured.			
I can write clearly and accurately, using a variety of sentence forms.			

Assessment

This section tests all the reading and writing skills that you have learned in this chapter to see if you are now able to apply them to different sources.

Read the extract below and complete the activities that follow. The extract is from an autobiography, *Coming to England* by Floella Benjamin. The writer describes her first experience of school in England, having moved from Trinidad in 1960.

Extract from *Coming to England* by Floella Benjamin

1 When I arrived at the school, many of the children rushed over and touched me then ran away giggling. I thought they were being nice to me. At that time I didn't realize it was because I was different, a novelty, something to be made a fool of and to be laughed at. The dingy Victorian building squatted in the large grey playground like a bulldog ready to attack. It was surrounded by high wire fencing, a hopscotch game was marked out on the ground and on one of the walls a bull's-eye pattern was painted.

2 Above the school's main door were some letters engraved in the stone; they were Latin words and I never did find out what they meant. Inside the school the walls of the long corridors were tiled halfway up, making the building feel cold. The tiles had been painted a mushy green, some of it flaking off where it had been scratched over the years by passing children. The ceilings and upper half of the walls were a dull beige colour and the floors were covered with worn and splintering wooden parquet. Off the corridors were separate, unwelcoming classrooms, each one with its own door, not partitions like the ones in Trinidad. But the desks and the blackboards were the same. I felt a little comforted when I saw them. At least there was something I'd seen before.

3 The structure of the day was also a familiar routine: lessons, playtime, more lessons, lunch and play, then ending the day with more lessons. The work the teacher gave us was so easy and simple compared to the work I was used to. Yet the teacher treated me like an idiot because she couldn't understand my Trinidadian accent even though I could understand her. I felt like a fish out of water. [...]

4   There was one game, however which I didn't understand at first but in no time at all I began to hate. The first time I saw the children play it, I knew it was wrong and cruel. I was standing next to the wall with the painted bull's-eye when some boys came up and spat strange words at me, words that I had never heard before but from their faces I knew they were not nice. They were words which told me that I was different from them and that they felt my kind shouldn't be in their country. I looked at them, confused and baffled like a trapped and helpless creature. What was 'my kind' and why shouldn't I be in the country I was brought up to love? The land of hope and glory, mother of the free. I began to feel angry and violent as I stood and watched their ugly faces jeering at me. But they might as well have been talking in a foreign language because I didn't understand the words they were shouting. I didn't let them make me cry though. I had learnt how to be tough during the time Marmie left us in Trinidad. When I got home and asked Marmie what the words meant, she looked sad and sat us all down and slowly explained that because of the colour of our skin some people were going to be cruel and nasty to us. But we must be strong, make something of ourselves and never let them get the better of us. That was the day I realized that in the eyes of some people in this world I was not a person but a colour.

This activity will secure your knowledge about **how to select and interpret ideas (AO1)**.

Activity 1

a Find four pieces of information in the first paragraph about the English school Benjamin attended.

b The second paragraph contains both explicit and implicit ideas. What do you understand about how Benjamin felt about her new school from this part of the text?

c Using your answers to the questions above as well as the rest of the extract, write your response to the following question:

> What do you understand about how Floella Benjamin was treated at school? Use your own words and quotations from the text to support what you say.

This activity will secure your knowledge about **how writers use text structure for particular purposes (A02)**.

Activity 2

a Write a subtitle that summarizes each of the four paragraphs.

b Explain how the writer organizes the text from one paragraph to the next and focuses on different elements.

c Write a paragraph explaining how Benjamin interests the reader by using the structure of her writing to show different aspects of her experience.

This activity will secure your knowledge about **how writers use language to create effects (A02)**.

Activity ③

a The writer uses the words 'mushy green' to describe the colour of the paint on the walls. What does her choice of language tell you about how she feels about the school?

b She describes the school as a building which 'squatted in the large grey playground like a bulldog ready to attack'. What effect does this description have on the reader?

c The writer uses the words 'the land of hope and glory, mother of the free' in the fourth paragraph. What is the effect of using these particular words?

d Find an example of a rhetorical question in the extract and explain its effect on the reader.

e Look at a student's response to the question: How does the writer use language to describe her experience to the reader?

> The writer describes an experience that is very negative when she arrives in England and goes to school.
>
> The language that describes the school suggests it looks bleak and unfriendly. In the first paragraph the adjectives she uses makes you think the place is unpleasant to look at.
>
> Her experience is like she is in a war. She uses language that links to violent things for example 'like a bulldog ready to attack'. She uses similes to show what the school is like and also how she felt about them when she says she was a fish out of water.
>
> She uses words to reflect that some aspects make her feel at home. It's not all bad though because she does see desks and blackboards that were the same as in Trinidad. She also says that the work was easier.
>
> The way she describes the people shows a bad experience. The teacher does not understand that although she can't speak the language, she is not stupid: 'she couldn't understand the Trinidadian accent'. The children are bullies.

Check that:

• the student mentions language in each paragraph rather than discussing the story of the text

• the student uses references from the text to support her points (for example, quotations) and then comments on their effect.

Now rewrite the paragraph, making changes to improve the answer.

This activity will secure your knowledge of **how to evaluate writing using references to the text (AO4)**. Note that in the exam, this skill will be applied to a fiction text, but the same skill can also be applied to non-fiction texts.

Activity (4)

a On a scale of 1–10, how sympathetic do you feel towards Benjamin?

Not at all
sympathetic

⟵━━━━━━━━━━━⟶

Very
sympathetic

1   2   3   4   5   6   7   8   9   10

b Look at the quotations below. Which one makes you feel most sympathetic to Benjamin? Explain why you have chosen it.

'I thought they were being nice to me.'

'But the desks and the blackboards were the same. I felt a little comforted when I saw them.'

'the teacher treated me like an idiot because she couldn't understand my Trinidadian accent...'

'That was the day I realized that in the eyes of some people in this world I was not a person but a colour.'

'I looked at them confused and baffled like a trapped and helpless creature.'

'some boys came up and spat strange words at me...'

c Read the final sentence of the extract again. Explain why you think this is an effective way to end the extract.

d This is what one reader said about this text:

'You can only really relate to Benjamin's experience if you have moved to another country yourself. Her writing doesn't help me understand her thoughts and experience'.

To what extent do you agree? Use quotations from the text to support what you write.

Read the following extract in which David Mitchell helps the reader imagine the experience of autism. He knows about this condition because his son has autism. He also worked with a 13-year-old Japanese boy, Naoki Higashida, to translate his world-famous book *The Reason I Jump.* Autism affects how people relate to others and their perception, through their senses, of the world around them. Some people have a mild form; others need lifelong support and care.

Extract from *The Reason I Jump* by David Mitchell

Imagine a daily life in which your faculty of speech is taken away [...]

Now your mind is a room where twenty radios, all tuned to different stations, are blaring out voices and music. The radios have no off-switches or volume controls, the room you're in has no door or window, and relief will come only when you're too exhausted to stay awake. To make matters worse, another hitherto unrecognized editor has just quit without notice – your editor of the senses. Suddenly sensory input from your environment is flooding in too, unfiltered in quality and overwhelming in quantity. Colours and patterns swim and clamour for your attention. The fabric conditioner in your sweater smells as strong as air-freshener fired up your nostrils. Your comfy jeans are now as scratchy as steel wool. Your vestibular and proprioceptive senses are also out of kilter, so the floor keeps tilting like a ferry in heavy seas, and you're no longer sure where your hands and feet are in relation to the rest of you. You can feel the plates of your skull, plus your facial muscles and your jaw: your head feels trapped inside a motorbike helmet three sizes too small which may or may not explain why the air-conditioner is as deafening as an electric drill, but your father – who's right here in front of you – sounds as if he's speaking to you from a cell-phone, on a train going through lots of short tunnels, in fluent Cantonese. You are no longer able to comprehend your mother-tongue, or any tongue: from now on all languages will be foreign languages. Even your sense of time has gone, rendering you unable to distinguish between a minute and an hour, as if you've been entombed in an Emily Dickenson poem about eternity, or locked into a time-bending SF film. Poems and films, however, come to an end, whereas this is your new ongoing reality. Autism is a lifelong condition. But even the word 'autism' makes no more sense to you now than the word 自閉症 or αυτισμός or ऑटिज़म.

[...] for those people born onto the autistic spectrum, this unedited, unfiltered and scary-as-all-hell reality is home.

Naoki Higashida

Both extracts on pages 68 and 72 deal with the theme of difference and understanding the experience of others. They were written by authors of different genders, nationalities and ages.

This activity will secure your knowledge of **how to summarize evidence from different texts (AO1)**.

Activity 5

a Using your own words, explain how the metaphor that begins 'now your mind is a room' helps the reader to understand how the autistic mind works.

b Select some words and phrases the writer uses to describe how his senses are overloaded.

c Look at how the reader is addressed in the extract. Can you find an example of where you are addressed directly by the author? Explain the effect of this.

d Using your answers to all the questions above, write your response to the following task:

> Using details from both texts, list the reasons why both subjects are distant from other people.

You may find the structure below helpful when writing your response.

Benjamin is distant from other people and her surroundings because:

- she doesn't have the same accent

-

-

-

-

Higashida is distant from other people and their surroundings because:

- his brain is overloaded as it cannot get rid of thoughts that enter

-

-

-

Key terms

First-person narrative: story or account told from the point of view of a character or one of the people involved, typically using the pronouns *I* and *we*

Second-person narrative: story or account told from the point of view of the reader, typically using the pronoun *you*

Third-person narrative: story or account told from the point of view of an 'outsider', a narrator who is not a directly involved, typically using the pronouns *he*, *she*, *it* and *they*

This activity will secure your knowledge of **how to compare writers' points of view (AO3)**.

Activity 6

a What sort of narrative perspective is used in each of the two texts, about Benjamin's life and about the experience of autism? (For example, are they written as a **first-person**, **second-person** or **third-person narrative**?)

b What is the effect of using these different narrative perspectives on the reader's understanding of the characters' thoughts and feelings?

c Select three uses of effective description in each text and explain how they support the reader's empathy (understanding and sharing of another person's feelings) with the experiences described.

d Using your answers to the above, write your response to the following task:

> Compare how the descriptive language and narrative perspective in these two texts influence the reader's response to the writers' ideas about being different from others.

This activity will secure your knowledge of **how to write clearly and effectively, organizing your ideas in a clear structure and using appropriate and accurate language (AO5, AO6)**.

Activity 7

Think about a time when you felt isolated or different from other people around you. Write a first-person account describing what happened and how you felt.

Remember to:

- make a plan before you start writing (think about possible ideas and note them down)

- structure your writing carefully (think about an introduction, grouping ideas into paragraphs and a conclusion)

- link your points and paragraphs together using connectives, for example: *then, next, after that, not long afterwards, eventually, the following day, within an hour, when I was five*

- proofread your work, checking spelling, punctuation and grammar.

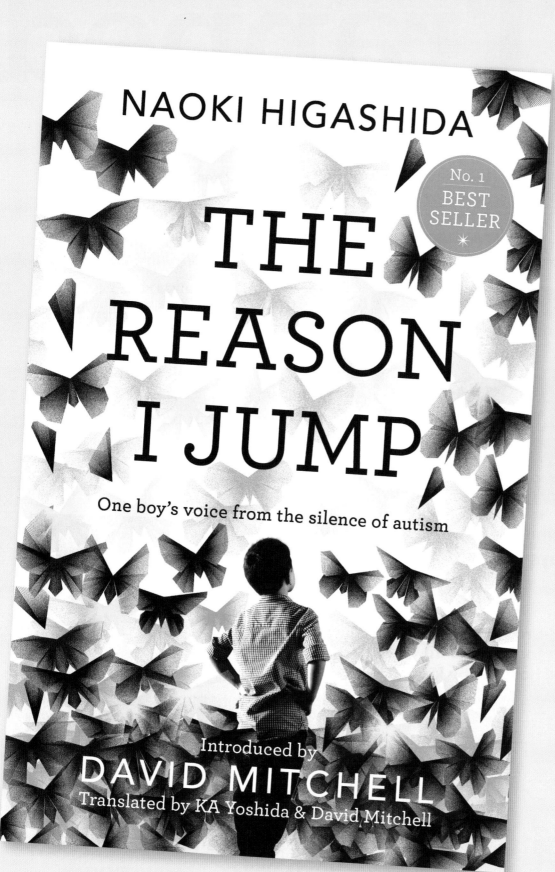

NAOKI HIGASHIDA

THE REASON I JUMP

One boy's voice from the silence of autism

No. 1
BEST
SELLER

Introduced by
DAVID MITCHELL
Translated by KA Yoshida & David Mitchell

3 Trapped

To be trapped is to be stuck in a situation that is beyond your control. It may be a permanent state. Or it may be that, with time and effort and perhaps a bit of luck, you can escape.

Some people find themselves physically trapped. Prisoners on death row in America, for example, are confined and know that the only likely way out will be death.

Other people find themselves metaphorically trapped, for example, by their own minds, other people or their circumstances.

In this chapter you will read a range of writing from different genres and across different centuries and encounter many different examples of being trapped.

Many headlines are made because of determined victims who eventually escape their entrapment. Do you remember any of these escape stories from the national news?

Chilean miners rescued after 69 days underground

Ohio Horror House: three missing women found after 10 years being held hostage by kidnappers

Great Escaper broke care-home rules to attend D Day commemorations in France

Skills and Assessment Objectives

All the reading and writing skills in this chapter are linked to the Assessment Objectives (AOs) for GCSE English Language.

Reading skills include how to:

- identify and interpret ideas and information
- select and summarize evidence from the text(s) to support your views
- examine how the writer's word choice influences the reader
- compare writers' ideas and perspectives
- examine how the writer uses structure to influence the reader
- evaluate what the writer does to make their writing successful, in particular the creation of tension.

Writing skills include how to:

- communicate imaginatively, in particular through dialogue
- communicate discursively, in particular by presenting a point of view
- organize your ideas so that your writing is well structured and accurate.

Activity

a Look at the more everyday experiences of being trapped above, and think about times you have been trapped. Identify three examples. Consider any of the following:

- events where you were trapped physically
- events where you felt trapped emotionally
- your life now and any aspects where you feel trapped or restricted.

b Decide which of your experiences of being trapped provides the most material to talk or write about. Join with a partner or small group to share this experience.

- Do you think you react well in such circumstances?
- Did you select the right choice from your three examples? Did you have enough to talk about?

c Which person in your pair or group do you think would be the most determined and quick-thinking in a real-life crisis of being trapped? What evidence do you have to support your choice?

Writing tip

Before writing in exam conditions, note down a few ideas on your given topic. Don't just start your writing with the first idea you have. You must assess which idea has the most material to interest your reader.

1 Survival

Aron Ralston was a mountain climber who became trapped under a boulder while hiking alone in the canyons of Utah, USA. Read the opening of a newspaper article that sets the scene for Aron's extreme story of escape. It was so extreme that it was made into a movie.

Extract from the *Daily Telegraph* website, January 2011

Home   Video   News   World   Sport   Finance   Comment   Culture   Travel   **Life**

127 Hours: Aron Ralston's story of survival

When the sun starts to go down on the canyonlands of south-eastern Utah in the American west, it bathes the vast rock formations and caverns in a deep red glow. It's beautiful.

But at night, if you're alone, it can be a cold and frightening place. Particularly
5   if you find yourself trapped in one of the deep ravines[1] that split the sandstone monoliths[2] in two. It would be difficult for anyone to hear you during the day – but in the dark, a cry for help would be met with only silence.

No one knows that more than 35-year-old Aron Ralston. In 2003, he had gone hiking, alone, near Robbers Roost –
10   an old outlaw hideout used in the dying days of the Wild West by Butch Cassidy. But while Ralston was climbing down a narrow slot in Bluejohn Canyon, a boulder became dislodged, crushing Ralston's right forearm and pinning it against the wall.

15   For five and a half days, he struggled to get free until he was forced to do the unthinkable. Using a blunt knife from his multi-tool, he began amputating[3] his arm.

[1]ravines – deep, narrow valleys
[2]monoliths – huge upright blocks of stone
[3]amputating – cutting off

The information and ideas contained in this article are both **explicit** and **implicit**. To show you understand a text, you are expected to **interpret** as well as identify the ideas and information.

Activity 1

Which of the following explicit pieces of information are found in the extract on page 78?

A Aron Ralston is 35 years old.

B His left arm was crushed by a rock.

C The area is beautiful when the sun sets.

D He was hiking in the east of America.

E Aron struggled to free himself for five and a half days.

F The area is cold at night but not frightening.

G Aron was climbing in Bluejohn Canyon when the accident happened.

H Robbers Roost was used as a hideout by Butch Cassidy.

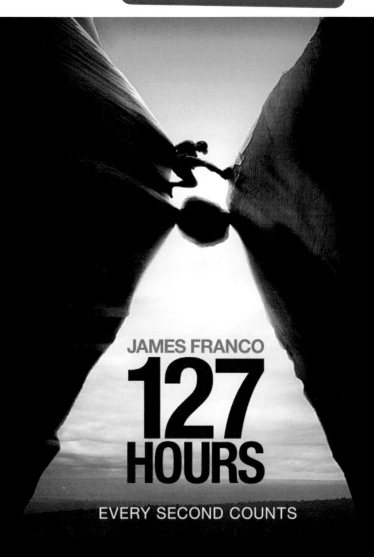

JAMES FRANCO

127 HOURS

EVERY SECOND COUNTS

Now you are going to consider implicit ideas and information. You will:

- make your points using your own words
- add supporting quotations from the text to prove your points
- comment on quotations to explain their significance.

Activity 2

Imagine you have been asked to write a summary of what is *stated* about Aron Ralston's situation and what is *implied*.

a Read the answers written by students Riley, Kasia and Charlotte on page 81.

b Read the teacher comments, also on page 81 and choose one to match with each student's answer.

c Order the students' answers from the best to the weakest.

Activity 3

Once you have completed Activity 2, write an additional point to extend Kasia's answer to this question. Demonstrate what you have learned about selecting implicit and explicit information and using a Point, Evidence, Explanation structure.

You could plan your answer using a table like the one below before writing it out in full.

Point	Evidence	Explanation

Reading tip 📖

The word 'suggests' shows that Kasia is considering what is implied. Other useful phrases include:

- 'This means…'
- 'This lets us know…'
- 'This indicates…'
- 'This implies…'
- 'This makes me think…'.

Student answers

Riley

When Aron Ralston becomes trapped and cannot get free, even after struggling for five and a half days, he has to amputate his own arm. He says he was forced to do the unthinkable.

Kasia

When Aron Ralston becomes trapped and cannot get free, even after struggling for five and a half days, he has to amputate his own arm. He says he was 'forced to do the unthinkable'. This suggests he is desperate to escape and can see no other way out if he wants to live. We understand that he is a really brave person to go through with such an extreme plan.

Charlotte

When Aron Ralston becomes trapped and cannot get free, he has to amputate his own arm. He had been hiking and exploring and then got trapped. Really he shouldn't have done this on his own as these lands were deadly and no one would be able to hear him if he had an accident which he did. He disregarded his safety and safety advice is very important. Everyone knows that exploring on your own is dangerous and clearly he didn't do his research and understand the risks he was under. People have talked about him as a hero and even made a film about him but really I think he brought it on himself.

Teacher comments

1

I am pleased to see both explicit and implicit information. You use a short quotation well and weave it into your writing. It is good that you comment on your quotation.

Targets: Try to focus your comment on particular words and explore what they imply in particular about Ralston. Add a second point to extend your answer to this question.

2

You have selected explicit information. I am pleased to see you are using direct quotations from the text – remember to use quotation marks to reflect that they are not your own words.

Target: Comment on the quotation and explain what it suggests about Ralston.

3

You use both explicit and implicit information in your answer and have understood the article. You have not kept to what the question is asking you as the second part of your answer focuses on your opinion about his actions. This is not relevant for this question.

Target: Keep to the focus of the question. Use Point, Evidence, Explanation so that all your points are supported with evidence from the text and you interpret that evidence.

Although Aron was an experienced climber, he made a huge mistake by not telling anyone where he was going that day. He knew there was no hope of rescue. The next part of the article shows his thoughts when he was trapped and how he finally managed to escape.

Extract from the *Daily Telegraph* website, January 2011

Home   **Video**   **News**   **World**   **Sport**   **Finance**   **Comment**   **Life**

'I realised early on that I was going to have to cut my arm off to get free but there was also resistance: I didn't want to do it,' he says. 'But by the second day I was already figuring out how I could do it, so in the film you see that progression:

5   trying to cut into the arm like a saw, finding the tourniquet[1], then the realisation that the knife was too dull[2] to get through the bone. That despair was followed by a kind of peace; a realisation that I was going to die there; and there was nothing I could do. It was no longer up to me. All I could do was see it

10   through to the end.'

After five and a half days inside the canyon, out of water, delirious[3] and hallucinating[4], Ralston had an epiphany[5]. 'I felt my bone bend and I realised I could use the boulder to break it. It was like fireworks going off – I was going to get out of there.'

15   Ralston managed to use his body weight to violently bend his arm until the boulder snapped his forearm. He then ingeniously used the attachment from his hydration pack - a bendy rubber hose that you use to suck water out of the pack - as a makeshift tourniquet, and began sawing and cutting through

20   the remaining cartilage, skin and tendons with his multi-tool.

[1]tourniquet – strip of material pulled tight to stop bleeding
[2]dull – blunt
[3]delirious – confused and feverish
[4]hallucinating – seeing things that don't exist
[5]epiphany – a sudden realization

Activity (4)

Using both extracts, on page 78 and above, write your response to the following question:

> Write a summary of Aron Ralston's experience of being trapped. Use your own words but also include quotations from the text to support what you say. You should consider:
>
> - how and why it happened
> - his thoughts and feelings about it
> - what the situation shows about Ralston himself.

Now read a second news article. It is also about being trapped. This time, the person involved is a young girl who worked in an industrial cotton mill in the 1860s.

Extract from a Victorian newspaper

A shocking accident, which will probably prove fatal[1], occurred at the Mechanics Mill, this forenoon. Annie McNeal, a girl about 15 years old […] in some unknown manner, got her hair caught in the 'back shaft' of a fine speeder[2] and was
5   drawn into the machine. The speeder was stopped as soon as possible but it was some time before the girl could be extracted, her hair and portions of her scalp having become wound around the machine. She was immediately removed to her home on North Main Street, and Dr A.M. Jackson was summoned. Dr Jackson found four scalp
10   wounds, the one behind the left ear being five inches long. A piece of the skull two inches[3] long by an inch and a quarter wide was also missing and the brain was laid bare but uninjured. It is barely possible that the child will recover, but it is more probable that inflammation[4] will set in with fatal results.

[1]prove fatal – cause death
[2]speeder – large factory machine that makes cloth
[3]inches – a measurement; 1 inch is about 2.5 centimetres
[4]inflammation – swelling

Activity (5)

a With a partner, discuss the similarities and differences between what happened to Aron Ralston and Annie McNeal.

Think about:

- the environment in which they became trapped
- how much control they had over the situation
- the efforts made to free them
- the involvement of others
- the final result.

b Summarize your findings by filling in a table like the one below.

Similarities and differences	Text 1 (Ralston)	Text 2 (McNeal)
The environment		
The victim		
How much control they had		
Efforts made to free them		
Involvement of others		
The final result		

Activity (6)

Using the work you have done so far, write your response to the following question:

> Summarize the similarities and differences between what happens to Aron Ralston and Annie McNeal. Use your own words but also quote from both texts to support what you say.

Both articles describe accidents and convey the shocking nature of the events. However the style of the 19th-century newspaper article is very different from the modern one. What they tell may have some similarities but the way they tell it is different.

Activity 7

Re-read the first two paragraphs of Aron Ralston's story on page 78, then read the article about the factory accident on page 83 for a second time.

a With a partner, select two words from those listed below that best describe the writing style chosen by the writer of each article. Use a dictionary to check the meanings of any new words.

descriptive   atmospheric   formal   emotive

cold   factual   everyday   sensational

clinical   persuasive   empathetic   vague

You could note your answers in a table like the one below.

	The writing style is:	Quotation
Aron Ralston newspaper article:	1. 2.	
Annie McNeal newspaper article:	1. 2.	

b Once you have agreed your choices with your partner, select a quotation to illustrate each of your chosen descriptions of style.

c With your partner, discuss why the two writers have adopted these different styles.

- How might they link to the purposes and audiences of these articles?
- How might their choices link to the century in which each article was written?
- Could their writing style reflect their personal viewpoint about the people and events they describe?

Share your ideas as a class.

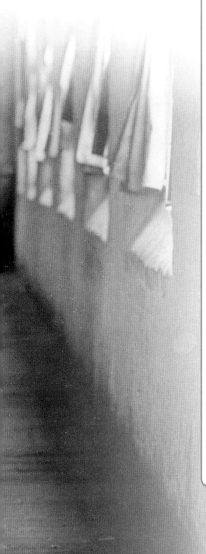

2 Let's talk about it

Skills and objectives

- To communicate imaginatively, in particular through dialogue **(AO5)**

- To organize your ideas so that your writing is structured and accurate **(AO6)**

Key terms

Dialogue: a conversation between two or more people. There are many reasons why writers use dialogue in their stories, including:

- to help the reader to understand more about the characters

- to show how different characters interact

- to move the plot forward

- to break up the action of the story

The text below is from a novel called *Eleven Hours*. Eleven hours is the amount of time the central character, Didi, is trapped with a stranger who hijacks her car while she is shopping in Texas. The **dialogue** shows the conversation Didi has with the man as he drives away with her trapped in the car.

In your own writing, every line of the dialogue should help the reader to understand plot and character. Avoid writing a whole story using mainly dialogue. Remember, the text below is just an extract from a whole novel.

Extract from *Eleven Hours* by Paullina Simons

'You could let me out.' She looked at him with hope. 'There's no harm done – '

'There is already.'

'No, not really,' she said quickly. 'I think you've made a mistake. You must think I'm rich, but I'm not really – '

'I don't think that, ma'am,' he said.

She pressed on, 'But if you continue, then you know, this will be a... a...' She couldn't get the awful word out.

'Kidnapping?'

'Yes,' she said. 'All you have to do is let me out right here. Please,' she added. 'Stop and think, think. Don't you know that kidnapping is a capital crime? In Texas, I think you get life for it.'

'They'd have to catch me first,' the man said.

'But they always catch the – ' Didi wanted to say *the bad guy.*

'Not always,' he said. 'Let them try to find us.'

Activity 1

a Look at the ideas below for how the story could develop. Which do you think would work best as a gripping next section for this thriller?

A Didi manages to get the kidnapper to agree to a hiding place, where she knows her husband will look for her.

B Didi spots a weapon in the car and manages to distract the kidnapper in order to get the weapon and use it immediately.

C Didi spots a weapon in the car and manages to distract the kidnapper in order to get the weapon and keep it for the right moment.

D A car park attendant, resembling a policeman, panics the kidnapper by knocking on the window. Didi manages to escape.

E Your own idea…

b Write the next three sentences of the extract to fit the beginning of your plot choice above. Remember to include a **reporting clause**.

c Discuss your plot choice and first line with a partner. Get feedback on your words, phrases and sentence structure. Is there anything you can improve?

Activity 2

a Look at the **verbs** the writer uses to show that a speaker is talking. The first one is circled for you. Make a list of these verbs.

b Do you think the writer varies her vocabulary to interest the reader?

c Write down some alternatives for the verbs she uses that work well in the context of each piece of dialogue.

For example:

'No, not really,' she said. snapped quickly.

When including dialogue in stories, there are punctuation rules that you must know. These make it clear for the reader who is talking and what they are saying.

Punctuation of dialogue

There are six main rules for punctuating direct speech. They are shown as annotations on the text below.

1 Speech marks, also known as inverted commas, always enclose the actual words spoken.

2 The words that are said must be separated from the person saying them. Here a comma is used. A question mark or exclamation mark can also be used to separate the two parts of the sentence if appropriate.

3 Every time a new speaker begins to speak, a new paragraph must be started. This means you do not always need to say who is talking. It can be obvious from the layout and flow of conversation.

4 All punctuation goes inside the speech marks, such as this dash.

'They'd have to catch me first,' the man said.

'But they always catch the – ' Didi wanted to say the bad guy.

'Not always,' he said. 'Let them try to find us.'

5 The first word spoken always begins with a capital letter.

6 The word after the speech in the same sentence begins with a lower case letter.

Activity ③

a Write a continuation of the dialogue on page 88 between Didi and her kidnapper, making sure you punctuate your work correctly. Use your chosen idea from Activity 1 as the focus of the conversation.

b When you have finished your dialogue, proofread your work. Check:

- what you have written is clear, correctly spelled and accurately punctuated
- you have varied your vocabulary and used a variety of reporting clauses
- you have made any changes that are necessary.

c Share your written dialogue with a partner. Ask for feedback on how far you have met the success criteria below. Make any improvements necessary.

Success criteria:

- Engage and interest your reader.
- Use a range of vocabulary.
- Punctuate accurately.
- Use a range of sentence structures.

Writing tip ✏

This extract uses direct speech or dialogue. Writers can also choose to use reported speech. This is when the writer summarizes the words spoken without directly quoting them in speech marks, for example, *She suggested that he could let her out.*

3 Under threat

Skills and objectives

- To evaluate how effectively the writer creates tension **(AO4)**

The director of a suspense or horror movie has music, sound effects, lighting and camera angles to help create fear.

A writer just has words on the page to create the same effects in readers' minds. This can be done through *what* he or she writes (the content) and *how* it is written (the style).

Content

Content can include:

- *setting*
- *events*
- *character reaction* – the emotional and physical results of the threat of danger.

Style

Style can include:

- *descriptive language* – creating atmosphere through dramatic words, phrases or language features
- *structure* – revealing events of the plot in a certain order to affect the reader, including plot twists and withholding information
- *sentence forms* – controlling the speed of the action through the length or construction of sentences for effect.

Read the opening of a short story called 'The Waste Land' by Alan Paton. A man finds himself trapped in a remote area by a gang of men. Tension starts building from the very first sentence.

Extract from 'The Waste Land' by Alan Paton

1   The moment that the bus moved on he knew he was in danger, for by the lights of it he saw the figures of the young men waiting under the tree. That was the thing feared by all, to be waited for by young men. It was a thing he had talked about, now he was to see it for himself.

2   It was too late to run after the bus; it went down the dark street like an island of safety in a sea of perils[1]. Though he had known of his danger only for a second, his mouth was already dry, his heart was pounding in his breast, something within him was crying out in protest against the coming event.

3   His wages were in his purse; he could feel them weighing heavily against his thigh. That was what they wanted from him. Nothing counted against that. His wife could be made a widow, his children made fatherless, nothing counted against that. Mercy was the unknown word.

4   While he stood there irresolute[2] he heard the young men walking towards him, not only from the side where he had seen them, but from the other also. They did not speak, their intention was unspeakable. The sound of their feet came on the wind to him. The place was well chosen, for behind him was the high wall of the convent[3], and the barred door that would not open before a man was dead. On the other side of the road was the waste land, full of wire and iron and the bodies of old cars. It was his only hope, and he moved towards it; as he did so he knew from the whistle that the young men were there too.

5   His fear was great and instant, and the smell of it went from his body to his nostrils. At that very moment one of them spoke, giving directions. So trapped was he that he was filled suddenly with strength and anger, and he ran towards the waste land swinging his heavy stick. In the darkness a form loomed up at him, and he swung the stick at it, and heard it give a cry of pain. Then he plunged blindly into the wilderness of wire and iron and the bodies of old cars.

[1]perils – dangers
[2]irresolute – undecided
[3]convent – place where nuns live

Key term

Connotation: an idea or feeling suggested, in addition to the main meaning. For example, the connotations of the word 'beach' might be sunshine or gritty sand, depending on your experience of the beach

Content

The writer establishes a setting where danger lurks. Look at the **connotations** of the phrases below from the story.

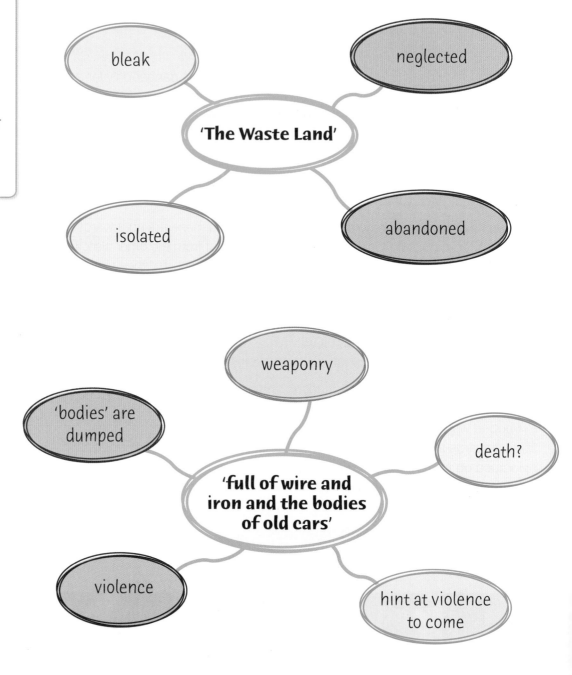

Activity 1

a Other details of the setting are gradually revealed to us as the story progresses. List four other details that tell us where and when the story takes place.

b Compare your details with a partner. Discuss whether each example adds tension to the story or what each suggests about the man's situation.

Activity 2

a Look at the events that happen to the man and how he reacts. Record these events and the man's reactions in a table like the one started below. Add some quotations to support your points.

What happens	Man's reaction	Supporting quotation
He thinks about running after the bus but it's too late.	He realizes he can't now easily escape and his body starts to physically react to the danger.	'his mouth was already dry, his heart was pounding in his breast, something within him was crying out in protest'

b Compare your table with a partner's. How do the events and the man's reactions add tension to the story?

Style

One of the reasons we can relate to the man's growing anxiety and fear is because of the writer's choice of words, phrases and language features.

Activity 3

a The departing bus is described as being 'like an island of safety in a sea of perils'. Explain how this **simile** works.

  i What is the bus likened to?

  ii What is the man's situation likened to?

  iii Which two of the following terms best describe the man's thoughts and feelings?

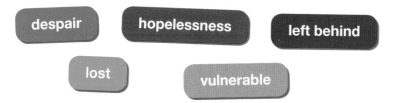

despair   hopelessness   left behind   lost   vulnerable

b The writer describes how the man hears the approaching footsteps: 'The sound of their feet came on the wind to him'. Why has the writer chosen this description? What effect does it have on the reader?

c Look at the final two sentences. What do the verbs 'loomed' and 'plunged' tell us?

d Choose two brief quotations from the extract on page 91 that you think convey the man's fear and tension. Explain why you think they work well.

Key term

Simile: a comparison showing the similarity between two different things, stating that one is like the other

Tension is also created through structure.

The writer uses:

- chronological order (describing events in time order) to organize the story
- a variety of sentence structures to vary pace and tension.

Activity 4

a Fill in a diagram, using as many boxes as you need, to represent the chronological events in the story. The first one is done for you.

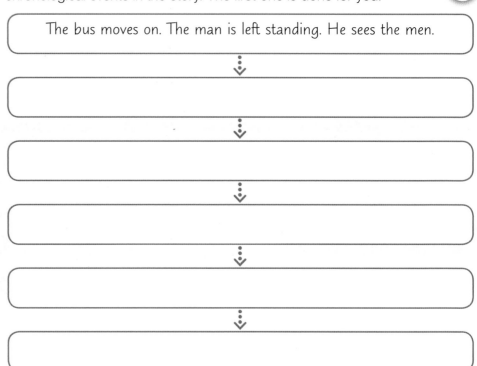

> The bus moves on. The man is left standing. He sees the men.

b Re-read this long **complex sentence** from paragraph 2 aloud:

> 'Though he had known of his danger only for a second, his mouth was already dry, his heart was pounding in his breast, something within him was crying out in protest against the coming event.'

  i What is the effect of this long sentence on the reader?

  ii Identify the verbs in the sentence.

  iii Which verbs do you think are most important in building a sense of fear? Give reasons for your answer.

c Re-read paragraph 5 aloud. Notice that it is built up of a series of actions. The writer uses a number of **compound sentences** to link these together.

- What is the effect of these compound sentences on the reader?
- List the four **nouns** in the first sentence? What do they suggest about the man's thoughts and feelings?

Activity (5)

Using all the work you have done so far, write your response to the following question:

How successful is Alan Paton in creating tension in the opening of 'The Waste Land'? Give your own opinion and quote from the text to support what you say.

4 A giant in science

- To examine how the writer uses structure and connectives to link ideas and influence the reader **(AO2)**

- To communicate effectively, structuring ideas to present a point of view **(AO5)**

- To write clearly and accurately **(AO6)**

Professor Stephen Hawking is a genius. His scientific achievements are world famous. But since he was a student, he has been battling with Motor Neurone Disease which has gradually paralysed him, trapping him within his own body. He has become so famous that an award-winning film was made about him and he even made a BBC guest appearance with David Walliams for Comic Relief in 2015.

Think about any people you know that think writing is hard work. Then consider how it would be to write whole books and academic papers letter by letter while only being able to move your eye to activate a computer – that's determination!

In the article on page 97, the journalist Lawrence McGinty remembers interviewing Stephen Hawking.

Stephen Hawking: 'I'm a scientist not a celebrity'

By Lawrence McGinty

1 Interviewing Stephen Hawking is a very strange experience for a journalist. Even meeting him is a little daunting[1]. He is, of course, a giant in science. So you know that behind those spectacles is a very sharp brain. But the Motor Neurone Disease that has afflicted[2] him for 50 years and left him unable to move means that there are no outward signs of that.

2 I say 'hello'. He cannot respond. He's just arrived in the lift at his office in the Department of Mathematical Sciences at Cambridge University. One of the two carers who accompany him all the time leans across his motorised wheelchair and holds Stephen's hand out, offering a handshake for him. I shake the limp hand and say hi again. No response.

3 When it comes to the interview, we have submitted our questions days before so he can prepare his answers in advance. He does this with a gadget in his spectacles which sends out a beam that controls his computer. He builds up sentences word by word, sometimes letter by letter and then sends it to the voice synthesiser that has now become his trademark almost. The robotic voice speaks his answers with a long gap between sentences. My problem is that I can't see his computer screen during the interview and I don't know when he's finished.

4 But it's sorted – everything seems to be sorted with Stephen. His carer who can see the screen gives me a nod when he reaches the end of an answer.

5 So yes, the stereotype of a giant intellect trapped in a twisted body is true. Stephen is very aware that's why he has become such a celebrity – his office is decorated with photographs of him with Barack Obama, Nelson Mandela and the Queen.

6 But he is above all a scientist. His place in scientific history is guaranteed by his discoveries in cosmology[3] – for example, that Black Holes don't suck in everything – they give OUT thermal radiation – heat. And whatever question you ask him, his answer is rooted in science. Is there a God? We are only intelligent monkeys on one planet among probably many in the Universe that might support life. A Creator is unnecessary to explaining our existence. Fracking[4]? We will need the gas when the lights start to go out.

7 Hawking is now 71 – when he was diagnosed with ALS (a type of Motor Neurone Disease) he was given two years to live. That was 50 years ago. He's still confounding[5] the doctors. He says he knows every day could be his last and he's dedicated to passing on his love of science – not just to his graduate students, but to everyone.

8 We leave Cambridge feeling that we've been in the presence of a unique, great man. Uplifted. And happy to have met a hero.

[1]daunting – intimidating
[2]afflicted – caused suffering
[3]cosmology – the study of the origins of the universe
[4]fracking – a controversial method of getting gas from under the ground
[5]confounding – surprising

Lawrence McGinty's impression of Stephen Hawking develops throughout the article. In his concluding paragraph he sums up by saying *'We leave Cambridge … happy to have met a hero.'* How he comes to this final opinion can be traced through the structure of the article and the changing focus of each paragraph. Key sentences and phrases, along with **connectives**, are used as structural devices to show the reader when his opinion is about to be shifted, moderated, contradicted or confirmed.

Key term

Connective: a word that joins phrases or sentences, such as *moreover, as a result, furthermore, in addition, not only… but also, because, therefore, consequently*

Activity 1

a What positive impression of Stephen Hawking is given in the first paragraph?

b Now copy and complete the table below which summarizes the structure of the first part of this article and how connectives are used to link his ideas together. You should:

- identify the topic of each paragraph
- finish the sentence starters, where given, to explain how the writer structures his writing
- identify the effect of the connectives in building and linking this ideas.

Paragraphs	Topic/focus	Key connectives and their effect
1	Hawking's brain and achievements	'But' links forward to paragraph 2 and shows that the writer is dealing with two different aspects of Hawking's life – his mind and his body.
2		
3	How Hawking communicates without speech	
4		'But it's sorted' links back to paragraph 3 and shows...
5		
6		The connective 'But' links back to the previous three paragraphs and the title of the article and shows...

Activity 2

a The whole text follows a cyclical (circular) shape, shifting focus through a series of time frames and ending with the same positive impression of Stephen Hawking as it started with.

> Question: How do you think the writer uses this structure to influence the readers' view about Stephen Hawking?

Which statement below gives the best quality answer? Give reasons for your choice.

1
> The writer links his paragraphs carefully using connectives to influence the reader.

2
> The writer McGinty tries to persuade us to agree with his point of view. He admires Hawking and uses the structure of his writing to show this.

3
> The writer structures his writing linking his points with connectives to emphasize that Hawking is primarily a scientist, but also an amazing man. He links his final paragraph to the title using the connective 'but': 'But he is above all a scientist'. This emphasizes his opinion about Hawking.

4
> The writer uses phrases that link backwards and forwards as well as to the title to create a well-structured piece of writing. Examples of these are 'But it's sorted' and 'But he is above all a scientist'. The structure emphasizes his view that Hawking is great.

b Select one of the weaker responses above. Improve it by adding evidence and explanation to explain how the writer uses structure to convey his viewpoint.

Activity 3

Using all the work you have done so far, write your response to the following question:

> How has Lawrence McGinty structured his article to convince us that Stephen Hawkin is a 'hero'? You should consider:
>
> - the title
> - opening and concluding paragraphs
> - paragraph organization and topics
> - use of connectives and links between different sections of the text.

Imagine you are a journalist who has met and interviewed a person you admire. Choose a famous person you admire and would love to interview. Write up your experience as a newspaper article. Use McGinty's article as a model. You might want to use the same opening lines to begin your piece:

> Interviewing [my hero] is a very strange experience for a journalist. Even meeting him/her is a little daunting. He/she is, of course, a...

When presenting a point of view, there are a number of things you need to consider:

- the **text type**, **audience** and **purpose** of your writing
- the opinion you are trying to convey
- a number of different points that will support that opinion
- the structure of your writing and how paragraphs link together
- effective vocabulary choices and language features.

Stage 1: Planning

Before you start to write, it is important to spend time planning what you are going to say and the order in which you are going to say it.

Activity 4

a Decide on the person you will be writing about. List some ideas about where you might interview them and what the setting might reveal about them.

b Decide on the point of view you are trying to convey about this person. What is admirable about them? Why are they amazing? Decide how you can reflect this in the article you are writing, mentioning details about their life and achievements.

c Look back at the article's structure you identified in Activity 2 on page 99, then plan the main focus points for your own article in a table like the one below.

Paragraphs	Topic/focus
1	
2	

Stage 2: Writing

Activity 5

Using all the work you have done so far, write your newspaper article about your chosen person.

Stage 3: Proofreading

Activity 6

a When you have finished your article you need to proofread your work. Check:

- your writing makes sense
- spellings and punctuation
- paragraphing and use of connectives to link them
- that you have followed your plan.

b Share your article with a partner. Ask them to suggest any improvements.

c Make any final edits to your work.

Progress check

In this chapter you have developed some key skills. Complete the progress check below to see how confident you now feel about applying these skills.

Key skills	Confident I understand how to do this.	OK Sometimes I understand how to do this.	Not sure I need to practise this more.
I can identify and interpret information and ideas.			
I can select and summarize evidence from the text(s) to support my views.			
I can understand how the writer's word choice influences the reader.			
I can understand how structure is used to influence the reader, in particular key sentences, phrases and connectives.			
I can compare writers' ideas and perspectives.			
I can evaluate how effectively the writer creates tension.			
I can communicate imaginatively, in particular through dialogue.			
I can structure a written piece to convey a point of view.			
I can organize my ideas so that my writing is clear and accurate.			

Assessment

This section tests all the reading and writing skills that you have learned in this chapter to see if you are able to apply them to different sources.

Read the newspaper article from 2012 below and then complete the activities that follow.

'I've got it nice,' says killer as he brags of easy life in jail

Eugene Henderson reports on a new TV documentary about prisons.

1 A SMIRKING killer has revealed the cushy time he and fellow 'lifers' enjoy behind bars in a controversial TV documentary that is certain to infuriate taxpayers. Callous Lance Rudge smiles as he tells of how enjoyable prison is for him, with his widescreen television, stereo and three meals a day. The unrepentant 24-year-old is puzzled why anyone would want to leave jail where he 'has it nice' and does not need to get a job.

2 Rudge was sentenced for the murder of disabled Gregory Butler at his home in 2007. He will not be released until 2025 at the earliest, but during the Channel 4 documentary filmed at Gartree prison, in Leicestershire, he makes it clear he is in no hurry. Last night, friends of his victim attacked the system that allows a cold-hearted killer to see out his sentence in 'holiday camp' surroundings. [...]

3 Sitting in his cell in a Stoke City shirt, Rudge tells viewers: 'In here you've got everything. You've got a stereo, a TV. You've got three meals a day. I've got it nice. I don't want it to change.' When asked what he thinks life is like outside, he says: 'Horrible. A nightmare to get a job. I wouldn't like to be out there at all now. I'd prefer to stay inside for a while, and wait until it calms down.' In the documentary, Rudge [...] tells the interviewer that being on trial for murder had been 'boring'. Rudge says: 'I fell asleep five times. It wasn't really the best impression to make but I couldn't help it. When I got sentenced I almost collapsed. But now I don't even think about it. Time flies by.'

4 Last night Staffordshire University lecturer Ken Raper, who as a former detective investigated the case, said: 'Rudge's words show there is no honour or loyalty among these people and just how little thought they give to others.' Alton parish councillor Tony Moult, who knew the victim, said: 'Rudge is lucky. If he had been tried before the Sixties he might have been hanged. It seems that prison is like a holiday camp. It is terrible for Gregory's family for it all to be raked up again.'

5 Last night the Tax Payers' Alliance called on the Government to tackle the issue of the easy life Britain's boasting lags have behind bars. Jonathan Isaby, the campaign group's political director, said: 'Any right-thinking person will find Rudge's attitude appalling and beyond contempt. Taxpayers expect to see prisoners being punished for their crimes, not given luxuries that many of us cannot afford in the outside world. Part of the regime should be about rehabilitation, such as instilling a work ethic in prisoners, something which appears to be lacking.'

6 A Channel 4 spokesman said: '"Lifers" provides insight into the realities of long-term imprisonment and the rehabilitative efforts of prison authorities.'

This activity will secure your knowledge about: **how to identify and interpret information (AO1)**.

Activity 1

a Look at paragraph 1 of the article. Select four explicit pieces of information about Lance Rudge's life in prison from the list below.

- He has all the food he needs.
- He has a stereo.
- He has a flatscreen TV.
- He has three meals a day.
- He enjoys prison.
- He lives a comfortable life.
- He has a widescreen TV.
- He is not being punished.

b Now look at paragraphs 2 and 3. They contain both explicit and implicit ideas. What do you understand about Rudge's attitude to prison life from this part of the text?

c Using your answers to the above and also the rest of the article, write your response to the following question:

> What do you understand about Lance Rudge's experience of prison from the article? Use your own words but support your ideas with quotations from the text.

This activity will secure your knowledge about: **how writers use text structure and sentence forms to create effects (AO2)**.

Activity 2

a Can you identify a time shift in paragraphs 1 to 3? How does the writer's use of this device help the reader?

b Several significant people are introduced in paragraphs 4 and 5. How does this structure strengthen the argument against Lance Rudge's views?

c The idea of prisoners having a TV, a stereo and three meals a day is repeated in the text. Identify other repeated ideas. Explain the effect of this repetition on the reader.

d Using your answers to the above, write your response to the following question:

> How has the writer structured this article to engage the reader? You could consider the writer's use of the following features, together with their effect on the reader:
>
> - time shifts
> - repetition of ideas
> - paragraphs and their topics/focus
> - introduction and conclusion.
> - other people's views

Writing tip

Before answering questions about structure, firstly identify the:

- text type
- audience
- purpose.

103

This activity about the newspaper article on page 102 will remind you **how writers use language to create effects for the reader (AO2)**.

Activity 3

a In paragraph 1, the writer uses the adjectives 'smirking', 'callous' and 'unrepentant' to describe Lance Rudge. How do these words influence the reader's views about him?

b What does the simile 'like a holiday camp' suggest about how prison life is viewed by some people?

c Re-read the sentence, 'Any right-thinking person will find Rudge's attitude appalling and beyond contempt'. What effect do the words 'appalling' and 'contempt' have on the reader? Use a dictionary if you need to.

d Using your answers to the above and any other examples of language that you find effective, write your response to the following question:

> How does the writer use language to make the reader interested in Lance Rudge's prison life?

Now read the following account of Charles Dickens' visit to Newgate Prison in 1836. Dickens describes a famous London prison that is very different from today's prisons. During his visit he meets a criminal who is due to be hanged the next day.

Extract from 'A Visit to Newgate' by Charles Dickens

1 We entered the first cell. It was a stone dungeon, eight feet long by six wide, with a bench at the further end, under which were a common horse-rug, a bible, and prayer-book. An iron candlestick was fixed into the wall at the side; and a small high window in the back admitted as much air and light as could struggle in between a double row of heavy, crossed iron bars. It contained no other furniture of any description.

2 Conceive[1] the situation of a man, spending his last night on earth in this cell. Buoyed up[2] with some vague and undefined hope of reprieve[3], he knew not why – indulging in some wild idea of escaping, he knew not how – hour after hour of the three preceding days allowed him for preparation, has fled with a speed which no man living would deem possible, for none but this dying man can know. [...] and, now that the illusion is at last dispelled[4], now that eternity is before him and guilt behind: now that his fears of death amount almost to madness, and an overwhelming sense of his helpless, hopeless state rushes upon him, he is lost and stupified[5], and has neither thoughts to turn to, nor power to call upon, the Almighty Being, from whom alone he can seek mercy and forgiveness. [...]

3 Hours have glided by, and still he sits upon the same stone bench with folded arms, heedless alike of the fast decreasing time before him. [...] The feeble light is wasting gradually, and the deathlike stillness of the street without[6], broken only by the rumbling of some passing vehicle which echoes mournfully through the empty yards, warns him that the night is waning[7] fast away.

4 The deep bell of St. Paul's strikes – one! He heard it; it has roused him. Seven hours left! He paces the narrow limits of his cell with rapid strides, cold drops of terror starting on his forehead, and every muscle of his frame quivering with agony. Seven hours!

[1]conceive – imagine
[2]buoyed up – kept cheerful
[3]reprieve – cancellation of punishment
[4]dispelled – driven away
[5]stupified – bewildered
[6]without – outside
[7]waning – fading

This activity will secure your knowledge of **how to evaluate writing using references to the text (AO4)**.

Activity 4

A reader has said: 'Dickens helps us to imagine the full suffering of a prisoner in Newgate.'

a List the items that Dickens chooses to mention in paragraph 1 that emphasize the man's suffering.

b Select two descriptive phrases that you think are effective in portraying suffering in paragraph 1. You should be willing to explain your choices.

c In the rest of the extract, the prisoner thinks about the fact that he will die soon. Copy and complete the sentences below to show you can identify his thoughts and feelings.

- The prisoner feels _____. This is suggested by the quotation: _____.

- The prisoner also feels _____. This is reflected in the quotation: _____.

- The prisoner thinks _____. This is suggested by the quotation: _____.

- The prisoner also thinks _____. This is illustrated by the quotation: _____.

Both the article on page 102 and the account on page 104–105 deal with the subject of people in prison, but they are written in different centuries and from different perspectives.

This activity will secure your knowledge about **how to compare writers' points of view about their chosen topic (AO3)**.

You will also **select and synthesize evidence from different texts (AO1)**.

Activity 5

a List three differences between the prison experiences of Lance Rudge and the man in Newgate Prison. You can use the sentence structures below if you want to.

On one hand, Rudge... while the prisoner at Newgate...

Lance Rudge experiences... On the other hand, the prisoner at Newgate experiences...

Finally Rudge's life is... whereas....

b The journalist writing about Lance Rudge conveys a critical view about modern prisons and Rudge's experience. Dickens describes Newgate Prison as bleak and he tries to convey the suffering of the prisoner.

- How do the writers use *language* and *structure* to convey their different views?

- Fill in the table opposite (on page 107), using the Point, Evidence, Explanation (PEE) technique to compare the writers' methods. The first box is completed for you.

Point

	Henderson's writing	Dickens's writing
Language used to describe the setting of the prison and the items available	Henderson describes the prison as comfortable and relaxing. He uses nouns to list the benefits of meals, TV and stereo. He uses the metaphor 'holiday camp' to criticize how comfortable Rudge is.	
Language used to describe the thoughts and feelings of the prisoners		
Structural features such as other people's opinions, time shifts, facts and opinions		

Example

Explanation

This activity will secure your knowledge of **how to express a point of view, organize ideas and develop them with detail (AO5, AO6)**.

Activity 6

Using all you have learnt so far, answer the question below.

'Prisons are a soft option these days. Prisoners should endure hardship; they are not there to have a good time.'

Write a letter to a national newspaper arguing for or against this statement.

Writing tip

A formal letter should have a date, address to/from, a greeting and sign off. In exam conditions you should indicate these elements quickly without wasting too much writing time on them. The body of your letter should be your focus.

Remember: Dear Sir/Madam = Yours faithfully.

Dear [name] = Yours sincerely.

4 All in the mind

Your mind is amazingly powerful. You have the potential to process huge amounts of information over a lifetime, retain thousands of memories and process millions of thoughts.

The human brain is the command centre for your whole nervous system and controls your response to all you see, hear, touch, taste and smell. We all perceive the world around us in different ways. To 'perceive' means to process the information we get from our senses and give it meaning. The same event may be experienced by different people, but each person may perceive it differently.

Most of us are confident that our senses are reliable – particularly our sense of sight. There is a common phrase: 'seeing is believing'. What do you think this means?

Skills and Assessment Objectives

All the reading and writing skills in this chapter are linked to the Assessment Objectives (AOs) for GCSE English Language.

Reading skills include how to:

- identify and interpret explicit and implicit ideas
- select and summarize evidence from texts
- analyse how writers use language and structure to create effects
- compare writers' ideas across different texts
- compare how writers present their ideas
- evaluate how successful writers have been.

Writing skills include how to:

- write for different purposes
- communicate clearly
- choose the right tone and style for your writing
- organize your ideas and use structural features.

By the end of the chapter, you will have been on a journey through the minds of many different people.

Activity

Look carefully, and in detail, at the image opposite on page 109. What can you see? Discuss it with your partner.

One title for the picture below is 'My wife and my mother-in-law'. Some people see an old woman; others see a young woman. Most are not able to see both images at the same time.

If writers want their readers to see things as they do, they must craft their words carefully to control readers' viewpoints. In this chapter you will look at how different writers craft texts to convey their imaginative ideas. You will also read factual texts about people struggling to control their minds and how it has affected their lives.

1   Fear and the mind

Skills and objectives

- To identify and interpret explicit and implicit ideas **(AO1)**
- To analyse how writers use language to create effects **(AO2)**

Some people watch horror films for pleasure. They like the adrenalin rush, holding their breath with suspense, and seeing familiar features of horror, such as ghosts, zombies and vampires in dark and dangerous settings.

Ghosts and vampires became very popular in literature in the 19th century through texts such as Bram Stoker's *Dracula* and Mary Shelley's *Frankenstein*. Time and time again, these stories have been made into different styles of films to horrify the particular audiences of their day.

Susan Hill is a modern author who has taken this traditional genre and developed it for modern readers. Her novel *The Woman in Black* was made into a film in 2014, starring Daniel Radcliffe, the actor who played Harry Potter in the Harry Potter films.

Read the film review of *The Woman in Black* below and answer the activity on page 112.

Extract from the *Guardian* by Xan Brooks, February 2012

★★★★★

The jury is still out on whether Daniel Radcliffe possesses the chops[1], nous[2] and nuance[3] to sustain a rewarding acting career away from Hogwarts. But credit where it's
5   due: the former Potter has taken a shrewd baby-step in the right direction with this busy, bustling ghost story that at times appears less indebted to the Susan Hill bestseller than the Haunted Mansion ride
10   at Disneyland. The plot is skeletal, a bag of bones, spring-loaded with booby-traps and wired to the mains as it shuttles Radcliffe's widowed young lawyer around Eel Marsh House, the obligatory 'old place cut off
15   from the outside world'.

Outside, in the cold, the Cold Comfort locals have secrets to hide. Inside, in the dark, the chairs are rocking and the stairs are creaking. There's a face in every
20   window and cobwebs on the chandeliers. I'll confess that James Watkins's exuberant joy-buzzer direction had me jumping in my seat and clutching pathetically at the armrest. All the same, I remain
25   undecided about Radcliffe, who endures each shuddering shock with a blank, stoic[4] fortitude that suggests a teenager taking his driving test. He passes, but only just.

[1]chops – looks
[2]nous – intelligence
[3]nuance – subtlety
[4]stoic – strong and uncomplaining

a Read paragraph 2 (line 16–28) of the film review on page 111. List four things that are seen in the film that are typical of the horror genre.

b A review text lists both factual information to inform the reader and offers the reviewer's opinion. Which four statements below best reflect what the writer implies in his article?

- Daniel Radcliffe's acting was terrible.
- He was frightened when watching the film.
- It's not particularly scary.
- The film was more of a comedy than a horror film.
- The film would have benefited from being more like the original novel.
- He was undecided about the quality of Daniel Radcliffe's performance in this movie.
- Taking the role in this film was a good career move for Radcliffe.
- The film has no story.

c Look at the rating given to the review of *The Woman in Black* on page 111. Write a paragraph summarizing how this rating links to the reviewer's article.

Many of the features of horror in the film review link to the supernatural, and a setting that is removed from normality. However, many modern horror books and films create fear by weaving it into more everyday situations. This makes us fearful by thinking that the unnatural can occur in the everyday world, rather than just one that is full of graveyards and dark old houses.

Many people have developed irrational fear in their minds of particular everyday things or situations.

Activity 2

a Look at the four everyday images on page 112. Did you or a family member have any irrational fears as a child? Perhaps you still have some? Spend a couple of minutes thinking, then discuss any irrational fears with a partner.

b Spend a few minutes looking at the picture below, noticing every detail. With a partner discuss the questions below. Make sure you have evidence to justify your views.

- What is happening in the scene?
- Where might it be set?
- Which aspects of the picture look exciting?
- Are the people having fun?
- Is there anything you find horrifying about it and why?

The following extract is from a 21st century short novel by Susan Hill called *The Man in the Picture*. Many features of this story are quite ordinary: an old painting that is bought, sold and passed between people. The painting reflects a real carnival celebration in Venice at a point in history, rather than a shocking scene from a horror film. And yet the picture seems to have power over everyone who spends enough time staring at it.

In this extract, a wife whose husband owned the painting tells the story. She lost her husband in the crowds in Venice at a carnival as they holidayed together and he never reappeared. One night, in her distress, she looked at the painting again.

Extract from *The Man in the Picture* by Susan Hill

In a single moment of determination, I took hold of the painting, turned it, and then looked at it with wide-open eyes. At first, it seemed exactly as before. It reminded me starkly of that horrible
5 evening and of the masks and costumes, the noise, the smell, the light from the torches and of losing my husband among the crowd. Some of the costumes and masks were familiar but, of course, they are traditional, they have been on display on
10 such occasions in Venice for hundreds of years.

And then I saw. First, I saw, in one corner, almost hidden in the crowd, the head of someone wearing a silk mask and with white plumes[1] in the hair and the eyes of Clarissa Vigo. It was the eyes that
15 convinced me I was not imagining anything. They were the same staring, brilliant, malevolent eyes, wishing me harm, full of hatred but also now with a dreadful gloating[2] in them. They seemed to be both looking straight at me, into me almost, and to
20 be directing me elsewhere. How could eyes look in two places at once, at me and at …

I followed them. I saw.

Standing up at the back of a gondola[3] was a man wearing a black cloak and a tricorn[4] hat. He was
25 between two other heavily masked figures. One had a hand on his arm, the other was somehow propelling him forwards. The black water was choppy beneath the slightly rocking gondola. The man had his head turned to me. The expression
30 on his face was ghastly to see – it was one of

abject[5] terror and of desperate pleading. He was trying to get away. He was asking to be saved. He did not want to be on the gondola, in the clutches of those others.

It was unmistakably a picture of my husband and   35
the last time I had seen the Venetian[6] painting, *it had not been there* – of that I was as sure as I was of my own self. My husband had become someone in a picture painted two hundred years before. I touched the canvas with one finger but   40
it was clean and dry. There was no sign that anything had been painted onto it or changed at all within it at any recent time, and in any case, I could no longer smell the oil paint that had been so pungent[7] moments before.   45

I was faint with shock and distress, so that I was forced to sit down in that dim little room. I could not explain what had happened or how, but I knew that an evil force had caused it and knew who was responsible. Yet it made no sense. It still makes no   50
sense.

One thing I did know, and it was with a certain relief, was that Lawrence was dead – however, wherever, in whatever way dead, whether 'buried alive' in this picture or buried in the Grand Canal,   55
he was dead.

[1]plumes – feathers
[2]gloating – being pleased in an unkind way that someone else has been hurt or upset
[3]gondola – long, thin boat found on canals in Venice
[4]tricorn – hat with brim turned up on three sides
[5]abject – wretched
[6]Venetian – from Venice
[7]pungent – strong smelling

Susan Hill uses language to paint a picture in the reader's mind of the night the woman's husband was lost. She crafts her words to imply that the picture itself is powerful and alive.

When writing about language, you must explore how the writer's word choices affect the reader. You must identify the *specific effect* the writer achieves. Just like the reader being a passenger in a car, the author is driving the steering wheel: guiding your route, your imagination and your reactions.

Activity 3

Read the quotations below and answer the following questions.

a Identify two quotations that you think best create **suspense and tension**.

b Identify two quotations that you think best create the **mood** of the carnival (both real and in the picture).

c Identify two quotations that you think best create *horror* for the reader.

A 'They were the same staring, brilliant, malevolent eyes'

B 'And then I saw.'

C 'The masks and costumes, the noise, the smell, the light from the torches'

D 'The black water was choppy beneath the slightly rocking gondola'

E 'In a single moment of determination, I took hold of the painting, turned it, and then looked at it with wide-open eyes.'

F 'his face was ghastly to see – it was one of abject terror and of desperate pleading.'

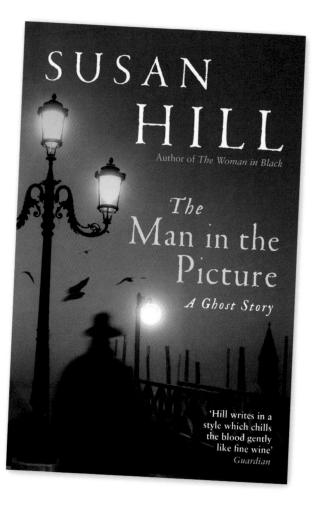

SUSAN HILL
Author of *The Woman in Black*

The Man in the Picture
A Ghost Story

'Hill writes in a style which chills the blood gently like fine wine'
Guardian

Of course, 'seeing is believing'. One of the ways that Susan Hill makes the story believable *and* horrifying is repetition of the idea of 'eyes': eyes that follow, eyes that are cruel, eyes that see what is real.

The author suggests that this is reality, not just imaginary, because the narrator has 'seen it with her own eyes'. She plays with our subconscious as we read; the apparent 'reality' of the situation has a horrifying effect.

Activity 4

Look back through the extract on page 114 and select four quotations that illustrate the theme of eyes and seeing.

Activity 5

Look back at the ten quotations selected in Activity 3 and Activity 4, on page 115 and above. Select a question which illustrates the language feature and effect in the table below. One example has been completed for you.

Feature and effect	Quotation
List of nouns to build up a picture	The masks and costumes, the noise, the smell, the light from the torches
Short sentences to create suspense	
Adjectives to describe the narrator's horrifying experience	
Adjectives to suggest a threatening setting	
First-person pronouns to help the reader empathize with the woman's frightening experiences	

Key terms

Adjective: a word that describes something named by a noun or a pronoun

First-person pronouns: *I* and *we* are first-person pronouns

When writing about language, try to use relevant grammatical terminology such as 'adjectives', '**adverbs**', '**common nouns**' and '**abstract nouns**' where you can, to help you explain the effects of language. For example:

> The writer describes the carnival, with lists of common and abstract nouns such as 'masks… costumes… noise… smell' to create a sense of energy, chaos and fear.

SPAG

Activity 6

a Make a collage of the colours, images and atmosphere created by Hill's description of the real and pictured carnival. Use pictures cut out of magazines or printed from the Internet. Select words from the text and label your collage with quotations to match the images you have chosen.

b Write a two-paragraph commentary to go with your collage, explaining how it reflects Susan Hill's language in creating a sense of fear in this text.

Key terms 🔑

Adverb: a word used to describe verbs, adjectives or other adverbs

Common noun: a common noun identifies a person, place or thing, but does not need a capital letter (unlike a proper noun, which gives the name of a specific person, place or organization)

Abstract noun: a word that identifies things that cannot be physically touched or seen, such as an idea, a state or a feeling

2 Places and perceptions

Skills and objectives

- To communicate imaginatively, adapting tone and style for a specific form **(AO5)**

- To use a range of vocabulary for effect and with accuracy **(AO6)**

- To evaluate a text and support with textual references **(AO4)**

You are going to write your own description using the first person 'I', just as Susan Hill does in *The Man in the Picture* on page 114. In your description you should:

- create a sense of fear or suspense

- focus on an everyday setting and consider how it can take on a horrifying aspect

- unsettle the reader's mind with the mood you create.

Activity 1

Look at the two images on page 119. Choose one as the basis for your descriptive writing.

Follow the sequence given in this lesson to plan, write and proofread your description.

Activity 2

Develop a word web to help expand your vocabulary related to the setting. Take a word which links to your ideas for a description such as 'fire' and write down all the **connotations** and **synonyms** you can think of. For example:

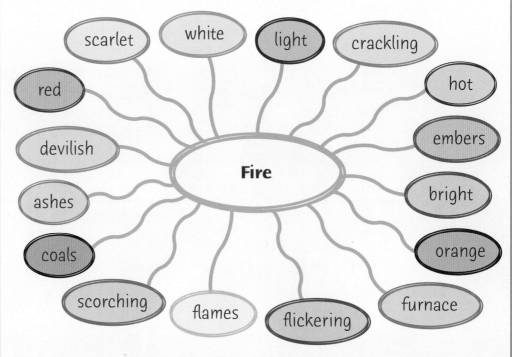

Do the same for other key descriptive words or ideas.

1

GUY FAWKES NIGHT

5TH NOVEMBER 2015

2

Key terms

Simile: a comparison showing the similarity between two quite different things, stating that one is like the other

Metaphor: a comparison showing the similarity between two quite different things, stating that one actually is the other

Word webs are useful when you are creating **similes** and **metaphors**. For example, you could use words from the web to describe a fire as 'a scarlet furnace of devilish flames'.

Activity 3

a Now write the first two lines of your description, immediately placing yourself in the setting of your picture selected on page 119. Use the first line of Hill's text as the basis for your writing, for example:

In a single moment of _____, I stepped into _____.

b Now, using all your preparation, write your description.
When you have finished, share your work with a partner. Invite suggestions for improving your description. Finally, proofread your work, checking your punctuation and spelling.

Activity 4

Swap your final work with a different partner. Then consider the following question in relation to the descriptive text you have been given to evaluate.

> How successful is the writer of the description in:
> - creating a sense of fear or suspense?
> - describing an everyday setting with horrifying aspects?
> - creating a mood that unsettles the reader's mind?

a Use a table like the one below to structure your evaluation. Use short quotations to support your views.

> Remember to make a few points and support them with quotations from the text.

> Remember to keep to the categories. You are not being asked to comment on spelling and punctuation errors here.

Categories	How this has been achieved	Areas for development
Creating a sense of fear or suspense		
Describing an everyday setting with horrifying aspects		
Creating a mood that unsettles the reader's mind		

b Now that you have planned your evaluation in a table, write your response to your partner's description in full.

One student's evaluation has been started below, as an example.

> The opening 'In a single moment of bravery' creates suspense because the reader does not understand why the bonfire night would be scary for the narrator until they find out that he has lost his parents.
>
> The description of the noise of the crowds and the fireworks 'cracking and hissing' help the reader to empathize with the boy's fear of loud noises. The description of his shivering adds to this idea. The writer has said he was shivering 'not from cold but from fear' so the reader understands the boy's reaction in his body.

3 Altering the mind

Skills and objectives

- To compare writers' perspectives and how these are conveyed **(AO3)**

- To write for different purposes, forms and audiences, organizing ideas **(AO5)**

People have been experimenting with the effects of drugs on their minds and bodies for centuries. Two hundred years ago, opium (a powerful drug, like heroin) was widely available in London, originally for medical purposes. It became popular among writers and artists of the time. Thomas de Quincey wrote about his experience of being addicted to opium. In his *Confessions of an Opium-Eater,* he writes about the pain he felt as a result of drug taking as well as the creative impact on his brain.

Extract from *Confessions of an Opium-Eater* by Thomas de Quincey

1   In the middle of 1817, I think it was […] a change took place in my dreams; a theatre seemed suddenly opened and lighted up within my brain, which presented nightly spectacles of more than earthly splendour. […] Changes in my dreams were accompanied by deep-seated anxiety and funereal melancholy[1], such as are wholly incommunicable[2] by words. I seemed every night to descend – not metaphorically, but literally to descend – into chasms[3] and sunless abysses[4], depths below depths, from which it seemed hopeless that I could ever re-ascend. Nor did I, by waking, feel that I had re-ascended. Why should I dwell on this? For indeed the state of gloom which attended these gorgeous spectacles, amounting at last to utter darkness […] cannot be approached by words.

2   The sense of space and in the end the sense of time, were both powerfully affected. Buildings, landscapes, etc., were exhibited[5] in proportions so vast as the bodily eye is not fitted to receive. Space swelled, and was amplified[6] to an extent of unutterable and self-repeating infinity. This disturbed me very much less than the vast expansion of time. Sometimes I seemed to have lived for seventy or a hundred years in one night; nay, sometimes had feelings representative of a millennium[7] passed in that time, or, however, of a duration[8] far beyond the limits of any human experience.

[1]funereal melancholy – sadness like that at a funeral
[2]incommunicable – cannot be expressed
[3]chasms – deep openings in the ground
[4]abysses – deep pits
[5]exhibited – shown
[6]amplified – made bigger
[7]millennium – a thousand years
[8]duration – length of time

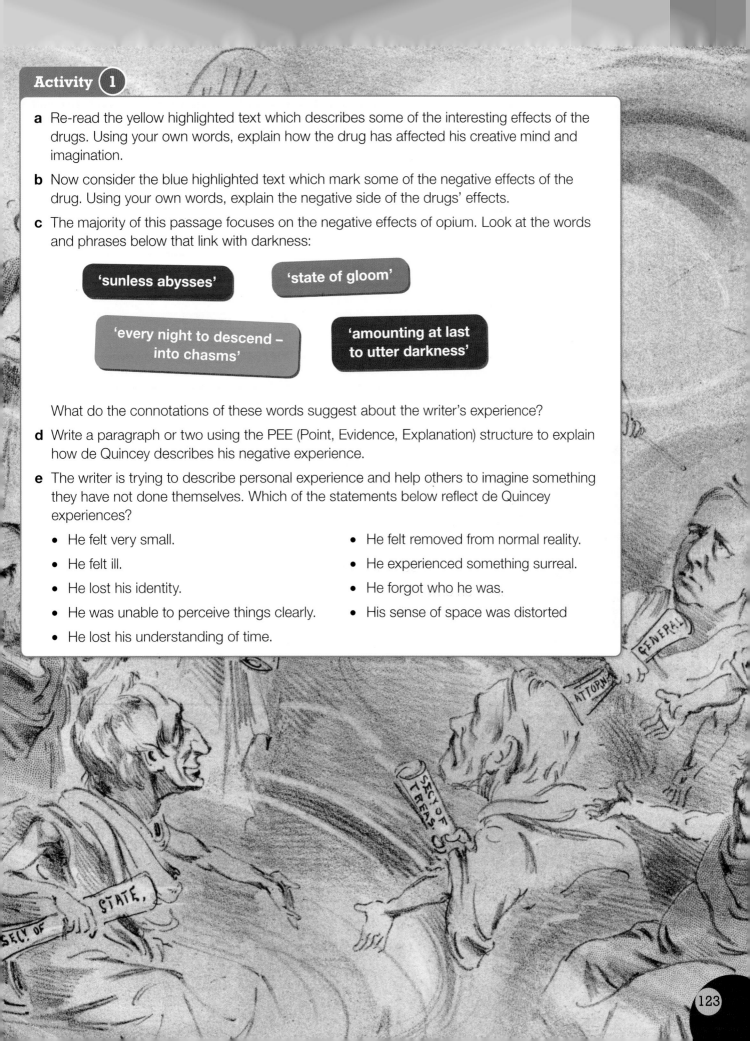

a Re-read the yellow highlighted text which describes some of the interesting effects of the drugs. Using your own words, explain how the drug has affected his creative mind and imagination.

b Now consider the blue highlighted text which mark some of the negative effects of the drug. Using your own words, explain the negative side of the drugs' effects.

c The majority of this passage focuses on the negative effects of opium. Look at the words and phrases below that link with darkness:

'sunless abysses'

'state of gloom'

'every night to descend – into chasms'

'amounting at last to utter darkness'

What do the connotations of these words suggest about the writer's experience?

d Write a paragraph or two using the PEE (Point, Evidence, Explanation) structure to explain how de Quincey describes his negative experience.

e The writer is trying to describe personal experience and help others to imagine something they have not done themselves. Which of the statements below reflect de Quincey experiences?

- He felt very small.
- He felt ill.
- He lost his identity.
- He was unable to perceive things clearly.
- He lost his understanding of time.

- He felt removed from normal reality.
- He experienced something surreal.
- He forgot who he was.
- His sense of space was distorted

In the 21st century, people are still taking drugs and writers are still trying to warn them of the dangers. One drugs advice group, 'Know the score', has published an online article on the risks of so called 'legal highs'.

Extract from the website 'Know the score'

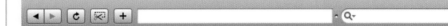

JUST BECAUSE THEY'RE SOLD AS LEGAL, DOESN'T MEAN THEY'RE SAFE

HOME

NEWS

FEATURES

1 Over the past 12 months the news has been filled with horror stories about people suffering from the serious effects of consuming so called 'legal highs'. The term 'legal highs' is misleading, as it implies these substances are safe when they are not and therefore these substances are often referred to as New Psychoactive Substances or New Drugs [...]

2 'Legal highs' are substances designed to produce similar effects to illegal drugs such as cocaine, cannabis and ecstasy, but have been created so that their chemical structure is different enough to avoid being classified as illegal substances. [...] Generally they are white powders, herbal matter or pills. The packaging can be colourful and attractive with hundreds of different substance and brand names. These drugs cannot legally be sold for human consumption, so are often sold as research chemicals, bath salts or plant food to get round the law. [...]

3 Like any drug, there is no way of knowing for sure what chemicals are in them. Unlike foods and other items that are for sale in your local shops, there is nobody testing these substances for safety, or checking to see what is contained in the packages before they are sold.

You don't know what you are getting

4 Many people have reported unpleasant effects to their physical and mental health as a result of taking these drugs. [...] Reported effects from people taking these drugs have included: nose bleeds, sickness and diarrhoea, black outs, short-term memory loss, severe[1] mood swings, anxiety, panic, confusion and paranoia[2]. They can also put a strain on your heart and nervous system. There are reports of people ending up in hospital, or dying after reportedly[3] consuming these drugs.

5 Like any drug use, use of new psychoactive substances can quickly spiral out of control. The long term effects can be serious, similar to other drugs and are not just physical. Your life can be affected in all sorts of negative ways – everything from losing your job to hurting friends and family or even worse. It's just not worth the risk.

[1]severe – intense
[2]paranoia – mental illness which causes distrust of others
[3]reportedly – according to reports

LEGAL HIGH

KILLER LOW

Legal highs are psychoactive substances that mimic the effects of controlled drugs although they have had their chemical structure changed.

Effects include seizures, comas, long term illness and in some cases death.

Don't take chances.
Get the full facts at www.westyorkshire.police.uk/legalhighs

Scan QR code for more info

Yorkshire & Humber CRIMESTOPPERS 0800 555 111

FORPOLICE NON-EMERGENCIES 101

WEST YORKSHIRE POLICE

This non-fiction article is structured in a way that guides the reader through the ideas. Each paragraph represents a separate stage in the development of the writer's argument.

A writer can structure an article or its individual points in various ways. One method is to move from a general statement to detailed information for each point.

| General information | ➤ | Detailed information |

Reading tip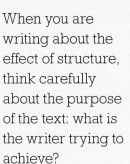

When you are writing about the effect of structure, think carefully about the purpose of the text: what is the writer trying to achieve?

Activity 2

The article on page 124 has five main paragraphs.

a Work in pairs to match the main topics in column 1 to the paragraph they refer to.

General topic	Which paragraph?	Detailed information
1. It is not possible for consumers to know what they are taking.		
2. It is common to experience unpleasant side effects.		
3. People's use of legal highs can become habitual.		
4. Recently, legal highs have hit the headlines.		
5. Legal highs are similar to illegal drugs but different in their composition.	2	They are white powders, herbal matter or pills. They can have attractive packaging and names.

b Now fill in the third column to identify three paragraphs that are structured by using a general topic followed by particular detail. One example is done for you.

c Texts to convey information are often structured in this way to make clear points to inform the reader and then illustrate them with further detail. Look back at the de Quincey text on page 122. With a partner, decide if you can identify the same structure in his paragraphs.

When you are comparing writers' ideas and perspectives, you must use the same structure. You must **summarize** and **synthesize** them, highlighting their similarities and differences. Start each paragraph with a clear topic. For example:

> The writers have different ideas about drug-taking and consider their topic from different perspectives. Thomas de Quincey writes about his own experience of taking drugs so his approach is very personal. He describes the personal feeling of having taken them as 'deep-seated anxiety and funeral melancholy'. However, the writer of the article takes a different approach and advises the reader based on the facts rather than personal experience: 'these drugs... can also put a strain on your heart.'

Look at the outline below of how to structure your own comparison of two texts you have analysed.

Introduction: summarizing each writer's views and perspectives on the topic.

Text 2 – Analysis of methods. How the writer presents ideas using:
- language
- structure
- **tone**.

Text 1 – Analysis of methods. How the writer presents ideas using:
- language
- structure
- tone.

Conclusion: Which writer is the most effective and why.

a Using all the work you have done so far on these texts, complete the planning for the following task:

> Compare how the dangers of drug taking are presented differently in these two texts on pages 122 and 124.

Look at the features of both texts below and identify whether they are demonstrated in Text 1, Text 2 or both texts. Tick the correct column in your table.

		Text 1 *Confessions of an Opium-Eater*	Text 2 *Know the score*	Both texts
Structure	Paragraph structures: general topic to detailed information			
Language	Written in the first person – personal			
	Written in the third person – impersonal			
	Discusses both positive and negative aspects of drugs			
	Uses rich descriptive language, including figurative language such as metaphors			
	Includes factual information			
	Uses second person 'you' to appeal directly to the reader			
Tone	Formal tone			
	Informal tone			

b Now look at the two student answers for the question below about the *Confessions of an Opium-Eater* text.

> Which do you think is better and why? Use what you have learned about how to compare texts and which aspects to consider in that comparison.

Maryam

Text 1 presents information on the dangers of drug taking in a number of ways. The writer paragraphs his information in separate points. He structures each paragraph with a clear topic sentence and then goes into detail afterwards to tell the reader about his experience. For example, the topic of the second paragraph is about how his senses changed and then he goes on to explain how he saw things differently. He shows the awfulness of taking drugs by using lots of descriptive language. For example he describes how bad he feels: 'into chasms and sunless abysses' which uses a metaphor to show that he is in a bad place in his mind. He also uses a formal tone to show the seriousness of what happened to him.

Saira

Text 1 is about the dangers of drug taking. The writer says that he experienced dreams that were amazing. He writes from his own experience so it's easy to believe what he says. But he seems to get very depressed because he says 'descent – into chasms and sunless abysses'. He describes how his senses were confused and he couldn't see things straight. He feels very disturbed by his experienced: 'Buildings, landscapes etc., were exhibited in proportions so vast'. He didn't feel any better whether he was awake or asleep. This is how negative drugs have been for him.

c Now imagine you are the writer of the stronger text. Write the second paragraph that follows on, identifying how the information is presented in the 'Know the score' text. You might like to use some of the connectives below to link your points back to your chosen first paragraph.

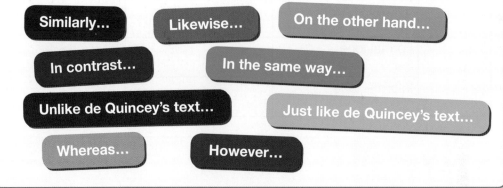

Similarly... Likewise... On the other hand...

In contrast... In the same way...

Unlike de Quincey's text... Just like de Quincey's text...

Whereas... However...

Now you are going to write an article of your own about the dangers of taking drugs. The article will be for a school or college newspaper. You will need to plan, write and proofread your article.

Here are some decisions you need to make in stage 1: Planning:

> Ideas – where will you do your research to get information and ideas? The Internet is always a useful source of information, but you might find leaflets locally, too. Remember to use your own words rather than lifting them from other texts.

> Perspective – will you choose to write personally or impersonally? Will you choose first or third person?

> Purpose – do you intend to argue with, persuade or advise the reader? Advising is usually done calmly; persuading is perhaps more engaging; arguing is often more passionate.

> Register – will your article be formal or informal to suit the reader?

> Language – will you use descriptive language or factual statements? Or might you use both?

> Structure – how will you link paragraphs to influence the reader? How will you order your points?

School News

Activity 4

Write an article for a student newsletter about the dangers of taking drugs.

When you have finished, share your writing with a partner. Discuss any changes you might make to improve your article.

4   Fighting the mind

- To identify explicit information and interpret implicit ideas, and to summarize evidence from different texts **(AO1)**

- To analyse how writers use language to achieve effects **(AO2)**

- To evaluate texts and support with evidence **(AO4)**

There isn't much in today's society which is taboo or just not talked about. However, issues to do with mental illness are still sometimes hidden. Many people find it too awkward, too embarrassing and too difficult to discuss openly.

Here, you will read two texts which deal with mental illness. The first is a news article about a woman who suffered from amnesia, which is a medical condition affecting memory. The second, on page 132, is an article about the impact of dementia.

Activity 1

Read the first article opposite. Consider the statements below and work in pairs to decide, according to the article, which four statements are true.

A The last thing Naomi remembers doing is her GCSEs.

B She couldn't remember how to use the Internet or a mobile phone.

C It has taken 17 years to regain her memory.

D When she woke up, Naomi had forgotten that she had a son.

E The amnesia was caused by the stress of doing her exams.

F Naomi is a single mum living in a council house with her son.

G Naomi used her diaries to help her remember what had happened in her life.

H She didn't recognize her own mum when she looked in the mirror.

Extract from an article in *the Daily Telegraph*, July 2011

Rare amnesia leaves mother with 17-year memory gap

1 Naomi Jacobs, 34, woke up in 2008 but believed she was just about to sit her GCSE exams in the summer of 1992.

2 The last thing she could remember was falling asleep in her bunk bed as a schoolgirl. She was horrified to learn she was living in the 21st century, and was even mother to an 11-year-old boy she did not recognise.

3 Doctors revealed that Naomi had been under so much stress that part of her brain had simply closed down, erasing many memories of her life.

4 She was left baffled by the internet, and flummoxed[1] by her mobile phone as she struggled to get to grips with modern life. Today, three years after waking up in the future, Naomi has finally regained most of her memory, and has written a book about her experiences.

5 She said: "I fell asleep in 1992 as a bold, brassy, very confident know-it-all 15-year-old, and woke up a 32-year-old single mum living in a council house. The last thing I remember was falling asleep in my lower bunk bed, dreaming about a boy in my class. When I woke up, I looked in the mirror and had the fright of my life when I saw an old woman with wrinkles staring back at me. Then this little boy appeared and started calling me mum. That's when I started to scream.

6 "I didn't know who he was. I didn't think he was much younger than I was, and I certainly didn't remember giving birth to him. I began sobbing uncontrollably. To say I was petrified was an understatement. I just wanted my mum. I couldn't get my head around going to bed one night and waking up in a different century."

7 Naomi, who was a psychology student before her memory loss, was told by doctors that she was suffering from Transient Global Amnesia, a form of memory loss brought on by stress. […]

8 Slowly she began the difficult task of piecing her life back together by ploughing through years of her diaries and journals.

9 Naomi added: […] "At first, I struggled to leave my home, and venture out into the world – but slowly, with the help of my family, I started to get used to the world again. Although it was traumatic, I'm really grateful for being thrown forward through time now. I've been able to follow my childhood dream of becoming a writer – and am currently writing my story."

[1]flummoxed – confused

As we live longer, more elderly people are suffering from a condition called dementia. This causes the memory to gradually fail. Terry Pratchett, the famous fantasy writer, suffered from dementia. He campaigned to raise the profile of this illness in our society, to get people talking openly about it and to get more funding to find a cure.

Before his death in 2015, Pratchett did get more media attention for the disease – perhaps because of his fame but also people were shocked that a man with such an amazing mind was going to lose control of it. The extract below is from an article in *the Guardian* that Pratchett wrote to support a campaign to help fellow sufferers.

Extract from an article on *the Guardian* website, May 2014

Terry Pratchett: Those of us with dementia need a little help from our friends

1 Dementia. The word itself describes shrinkage of the brain, the process of abnormal proteins clinging to the spongy masses of our cranium[1] that we rely on to think and speak. However, the real and tangible[2] meaning of the word will be different to everyone living with the condition. For some, they might struggle in a supermarket with finding the right change. That nagging voice in their head willing them to understand the difference between a 5p piece and £1 and yet their brain refusing to help them. Or they might lose patience with friends or family, struggling to follow conversations.

2 For me, living with posterior cortical atrophy[3] began when I noticed the precision of my touch-typing getting progressively worse and my spelling starting to slip. For an author, what could be worse? And so I sought help, and will always be the loud and proud type to speak my mind and admit I'm having trouble. But there are many people with dementia too worried about failing with simple tasks in public to even step out of the house. I believe this is because simple displays of kindness often elude[4] the best of us in these manic modern days of ours.

3 Ultimately, research is the answer. While talented scientists beaver away at finding a cure, this campaign holds a mirror up to us all – forcing us to realise we can do more in our everyday lives to help. Look past that mirror, maybe even through the wall, to the house of your next-door neighbour. Maybe it's an older lady, albeit[5] only in her 60s, who you haven't recently seen popping to the shops as usual. You notice that she's forgotten to collect her milk from the doorstep, and that when you last stopped to chat she seemed confused and couldn't follow what you were saying. Think of how you might be able to help her – there are little things you could do to support her and let her know she's not alone. There are hundreds of thousands of us out there living with dementia who – to paraphrase[6] the song in the advert – every now and again really could do with a little help from a friend.

[1]cranium – skull
[2]tangible – practical
[3]atrophy – decay

[4]elude – escape
[5]albeit – though
[6]paraphrase – explain in different words

Throughout the article on page 132, Terry Pratchett's purpose is clearly to persuade readers. He uses **emotive language** to make the reader feel strongly about his subject, hoping to persuade them to do something to help.

Activity 2

a For each of the following examples, analyse the emotive effect you think the writer wants the reader to feel:

> 'struggling to follow conversations'

> 'manic modern days of ours'

> 'talented scientists beaver away'

> 'hundreds of thousands of us out there'

b Pratchett begins with a definition of dementia, using technical terms. What is the effect of using this sort of language?

c The writer uses a metaphor of a mirror in the third paragraph. Explain how the metaphor works and its effect on the reader.

Terry Pratchett uses a very simple structure in this article:

Cause Effect

Problem Solution

The sequence of ideas moves from the subject of dementia (the cause) to how it impacts on older people (the effect). Then the writer identifies how those people struggle (the problem), before explaining how scientists and friends can help (the solution). These are links you will often find in articles where the writer's purpose is to argue or persuade.

Activity 3

a With a partner, think of a suitable subheading for each of the three paragraphs.

b How does the narrative perspective differ in each paragraph?

- Is it **subjective** or **objective**?
- What is the effect on the reader?

Using all the work you have done so far, answer the following question:

> How successful is Terry Pratchett in persuading readers that people with dementia need 'a little help from a friend'?
>
> Remember to comment on the writer's use of language, structure and tone.

Progress check

In this chapter you have developed some key skills. Complete the progress check below to see how confident you now feel about applying these skills.

Key skills	Confident I understand how to do this.	OK Sometimes I understand how to do this.	Not sure I need to practise this more.
I can identify and interpret explicit and implicit ideas.			
I can select and summarize evidence from texts.			
I can analyse how writers use language and structure to create effects.			
I can compare writers' ideas and their presentation of ideas across different texts.			
I can evaluate how successful writers have been.			
I can write for different purposes, choosing the right tone and style.			
I can organize my ideas and use structural features to communicate clearly.			

Assessment

This section tests all the reading and writing skills that you have learned in this chapter to see if you are able to apply them to different sources.

Read the extract below and complete the activities that follow.

The extract is from a non-fiction book called *The Psychopath Test* by journalist Jon Ronson. Jon is taken by Brian, his guide, to meet a man called Tony, who is being held in a psychiatric hospital (for mentally ill patients) at Broadmoor, a secure hospital that contains many dangerous criminals.

Extract from *The Psychopath Test* by Jon Ronson

The Broadmoor visitors' centre was painted in the calming hues[1] of a municipal leisure complex – all peach and pink and pine. The prints on the walls were mass-produced pastel paintings of
5 French doors opening onto beaches at sunrise. The building was called the Wellness Centre. I had caught the train here from London. I began to yawn uncontrollably around Kempton Park. This tends to happen to me in the face of stress.
10 Apparently dogs do it too. They yawn when anxious.

Brian picked me up at the station and we drove the short distance to Broadmoor. We passed through two cordons[2] – 'Do you have a
15 mobile phone?' the guard asked me at the first. 'Recording equipment? A cake with a hacksaw hidden inside it? A ladder?' – and then on through gates cut out of high-security fence after fence after fence.

20 'I think Tony's the only person in the whole DSPD unit to have been given the privilege of meeting people in the Wellness Centre,' Brian said as we waited.

'What does DSPD stand for?' I asked.

'Dangerous and Severe Personality Disorder,' said 25 Brian.

There was a silence.

'Is Tony in the part of Broadmoor that houses the *most dangerous* people?' I asked.

'Crazy, isn't it?' laughed Brian. 30

Patients began drifting in to sit with their loved ones at tables and chairs that had been fixed to the ground. They all looked quite similar to each other, quite docile[3] and sad-eyed.

'They're medicated,' whispered Brian. 35

They were mostly overweight, wearing loose, comfortable T-shirts and elasticated sweatpants. There probably wasn't much to do in Broadmoor but eat.

I wondered if any of them were famous. […] 40

'Ah! Here's Tony now!' said Brian.

I looked across the room. A man in his late twenties was walking towards us. He wasn't shuffling like the others had. He was sauntering[4]. His arm was outstretched. He wasn't wearing sweatpants. He 45 was wearing a pinstripe jacket and trousers. He looked like a young businessman trying to make his way in the world, someone who wanted to show everyone that he was very, very sane.

50 And of course, as I watched him approach our table, I wondered if the pinstripe was a clue that he was sane or a clue that he wasn't.

We shook hands.

'I'm Tony,' he said. He sat down.

55 'So Brian says you faked your way in here,' I said.

'That's exactly right,' said Tony.

He had the voice of a normal, nice, eager-to-help young man.

'I'd committed GBH [grievous bodily harm],' he
60 said. 'After they arrested me I sat in my cell and

I thought, "I'm looking at five to seven years." So I asked the other prisoners what to do. They said, "Easy! Tell them you're mad! They'll put you in a county hospital. You'll have Sky TV and a PlayStation. Nurses will bring you pizzas." But they 65 didn't send me to some cushy hospital. They sent me to [...] BROADMOOR.'

How long ago was this?' I asked.

'Twelve years ago,' said Tony.

I involuntarily[5] grinned. 70

Tony grinned back.

[1]hues – colours
[2]cordons – barriers to make a secure area
[3]docile – willing to do what is asked
[4]sauntering – walking slowly and casually
[5]involuntarily – not deliberately

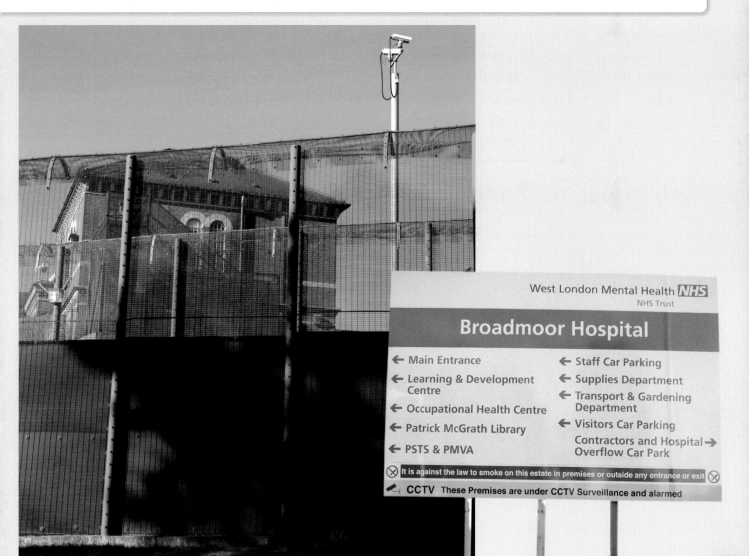

West London Mental Health **NHS**
NHS Trust

Broadmoor Hospital

← Main Entrance   ← Staff Car Parking
← Learning & Development   ← Supplies Department
  Centre   ← Transport & Gardening
← Occupational Health Centre   Department
← Patrick McGrath Library   ← Visitors Car Parking
← PSTS & PMVA   Contractors and Hospital →
                               Overflow Car Park

⊗ It is against the law to smoke on this estate in premises or outside any entrance or exit ⊗
CCTV These Premises are under CCTV Surveillance and alarmed

This activity will secure your knowledge about **how to identify and interpret information (AO1)**.

Activity 1

a From the first two paragraphs of text, select four pieces of information about Broadmoor Psychiatric Hospital.

b What impression does the writer give of the patients in Broadmoor?

c How do you think the writer feels about visiting Broadmoor?

This activity will secure your knowledge about **how writers use language and sentence forms to create effects (AO2)**.

Activity 2

a What is the effect of the writer describing the visitors' centre as 'all peach and pink and pine'?

b Find two examples where the writer has adopted a comic tone and explain the effect on the reader of using humour in the text.

c The writer uses a range of sentence forms. Select an example from the text and explain the effect on the reader.

d Using your answers to the above and any other examples of language that you find effective, answer the following question:

How does the writer use language to create a light-hearted tone about this serious place?

Now read the second extract opposite. It is a newspaper article written by Fanny Fern, a 19th-century journalist. A 'lunatic asylum' was the term used in the 1800s for a psychiatric hospital.

Newspaper article by Fanny Fern in the 19th century

My verdict after visiting a Lunatic Asylum is, […] what an immense improvement has modern humanity effected in the treatment of these unfortunates[1]! What an advance upon the diabolical[2] cruelty of blows and stripes, and iron cages, and nothing to do, and no room to do it in! Now, we
5 have the elegant, spacious, well-ventilated and attractive building, surrounded with scenes of natural grandeur and beauty […]. One draws a long breath of relief to see them, under the eye of a watchful superintendent, raking hay in the sweet, fresh meadows, or walking about in the beautiful garden […].

How affecting, too, is the child-like confidence with which they approach a
10 perfect stranger, to tell the sorrow that is eating their lives away. One sat at the window of a handsome room, watching with a smiling countenance[3] the gravel-walk that led to the building. As I entered, she said, "I don't know when he will come; he said he would come and take me away, and I am going to sit here and wait for him;" and she turned again to the window and looked far off into the
15 bright sunshine, and folded her hands in her lap in cheerful expectancy.

As the key was turned in one of the wards a woman rushed to the door, and said fiercely to the doctor, "Let me out, I say!" He calmly barred the entrance with his arm, and laying one hand soothingly on her shoulder, replied, "By and by – wait a little – won't you?" Her countenance grew placid[4]; and she replied
20 coaxingly, "Well, let me have one little peep out there then." – "Yes," said he, "you may go so far," pointing to a designated limit, but not accompanying her. She walked out delightedly, took a survey of the hall, and promptly returning, said, "I wanted my father, but I see he is not there." It seemed so humane[5] to satisfy the poor creature, even though she might be a prey[6] to some other
25 fantasy the next minute.

It is a very curious sight, these lunatics – men and women, preparing food in the perfectly-arranged kitchen. One's first thought, to be sure, is some possibly noxious[7] ingredient that might be cunningly mixed in the viands[8]; but further observation showed the impossibility of this, under the rigid surveillance[9]
30 exercised. In fact I began to doubt whether our guide was not humbugging[10] us as to the real state of these people's intellects; particularly as some of them
35 employed in the grounds, as we went out, took off their hats, and smiled and bowed to us in the most approved manner.

[1]unfortunates – vulnerable people
[2]diabolical – very wicked
[3]countenance – face
[4]placid – calm
[5]humane – tender, in a way to cause the least harm
[6]prey – vulnerable
[7]noxious – unpleasant and harmful
[8]viands – food
[9]surveillance – close watch
[10]humbugging – misleading

This activity will secure your knowledge about **how writers use structure (AO2)**.

Activity 3

a Write a summary sentence for each of the four paragraphs.

b Identify how and where the writer's perspective shifts as the article progresses.

c Choose either the first or the last sentence in the text and explain its effect on the reader.

d Using your answers to the above and any other examples of structure that you find effective, answer the following question:

How does the writer use structure to engage the reader's interest?

This activity will secure your understanding of **how to evaluate a text (AO4)**.

Activity 4

a Look at the language and the use of contrast in the first paragraph. How has the writer revealed a particular view of the lunatic asylum?

b What tone do you think the writer has adopted? Choose the best option below. Use a dictionary if you need to.

- sympathetic

- aggressive

- judgemental

- factual

- emotional

- naive

Select three quotations which you think demonstrate that tone and analyse what effect this tone has on the reader.

c What is the effect of including the conversation between one of the patients and the doctor in the third paragraph?

d Using your answers to the above, and any other aspect of the text which you think is appropriate, answer the following question:

> 'Fanny Fern presents a view of the asylum which is almost too good to be true.' How far do you agree with this statement?

Both of these texts (on pages 134 and 137) describe a visit to a psychiatric hospital, but they were written in different centuries and from different perspectives.

The activity will secure your understanding of **how to summarize evidence from different texts (AO1)**.

Activity 5

Using details and quotations from both texts, summarize the differences between the attitudes of the two writers towards their experiences at the psychiatric hospitals.

This activity will secure your understanding of **how to compare texts (AO3)**.

Activity 6

Compare how the patients are presented differently in the two texts.
Remember to comment on the writers' use of language, structure and tone.

This activity will secure your understanding of **how to apply writing skills (AO5, AO6)**.

Activity 7

a Write a description inspired by the picture on this page or describe an old person you know well.

b Write a persuasive article for a local newspaper arguing either for or against this statement:

'Old people are useless. They should all be kept in care homes.'

5 Town and country

Our daily experience of Britain is coloured by whether we live in the town or the country. Do you remember the famous story of *The Town Mouse and the Country Mouse*? You may have read it as a young child. The town mouse was proud of his richer lifestyle but when the country mouse visited he couldn't bear the pace and the danger. Many of us still associate ourselves with one or the other of those famous little characters!

Wherever you live now, the time will come when you can choose your own place to live and work. Do you long to escape the noise, pollution and bustle of the town to enjoy the peace of the countryside? Or are you fed up of the boredom and inconvenience of being stuck in your village and crave the buzz of the city?

This chapter will take you to visit the cities and countryside featured in various novels. You will see the very different worlds of the characters who live there.

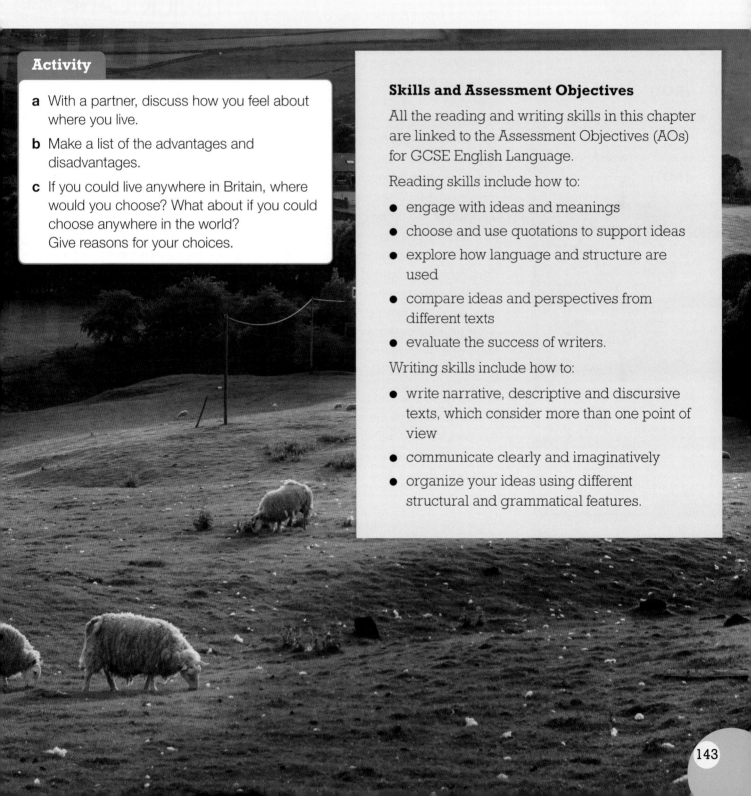

Activity

a With a partner, discuss how you feel about where you live.

b Make a list of the advantages and disadvantages.

c If you could live anywhere in Britain, where would you choose? What about if you could choose anywhere in the world?
Give reasons for your choices.

Skills and Assessment Objectives

All the reading and writing skills in this chapter are linked to the Assessment Objectives (AOs) for GCSE English Language.

Reading skills include how to:

- engage with ideas and meanings
- choose and use quotations to support ideas
- explore how language and structure are used
- compare ideas and perspectives from different texts
- evaluate the success of writers.

Writing skills include how to:

- write narrative, descriptive and discursive texts, which consider more than one point of view
- communicate clearly and imaginatively
- organize your ideas using different structural and grammatical features.

1 Brick Lane

The extracts below are from a novel called *Brick Lane* written in 2003. It is about a girl, Nazneen, who travels from her home in Bangladesh to live in this real street in east London. The extract describes her first visit into the city.

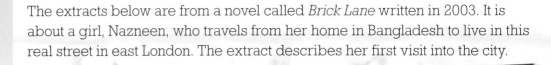

Extract from *Brick Lane* by Monica Ali

Outside, small patches of mist bearded the lamp-posts and a gang of pigeons turned weary circles on the grass like prisoners in an exercise yard. A woman hurried past with a small child in her arms. The child screamed and kicked
5 its legs against the kidnapper. The woman produced a plastic rattle with which to gag her victim. Nazneen pulled the end of her sari over her hair. At the main road she looked both ways, and then went left. Two men were dragging furniture out of a junk shop to display on the pavement. One of them went inside and came out again with a
10 wheelchair. He tied a chain around it and padlocked it to an armchair as if arranging a three-legged furniture race. Nazneen changed her mind and turned around. She walked until she reached the big crossroads and waited at the kerb while the traffic roared from one direction and then the next. Twice she stepped into the road and drew
15 back again. To get to the other side of the street without being hit by a car was like walking out in the monsoon[1] and hoping to dodge the raindrops. A space opened up before her. God is great, said Nazneen under her breath. She ran.

A horn blared like an ancient muezzin[2], ululating[3] painfully, stretching
20 his vocal cords to the limit. She stopped and the car swerved. Another car skidded to a halt in front of her and the driver got out and began to shout. She ran again and turned into a side street, then off again to the right onto Brick Lane.

***

Then she turned off at random, began to run, limped for a while to
25 save her ankle, and thought she had come in a circle. The buildings seemed familiar. She sensed rather than saw, because she had taken care not to notice. But now she slowed down and looked around her. She looked up at a building as she passed. It was constructed almost entirely of glass, with a few thin rivets of steel holding it together. The
30 entrance was like a glass fan, rotating slowly, sucking people in, wafting others out. Inside, on a raised dais[4], a woman behind a glass desk crossed and uncrossed her thin legs. She wedged a telephone receiver between her ear and shoulder and chewed on a finger-nail. Nazneen

35   craned her head back and saw that the glass above became dark as a night
pond. The building was without end. Above, somewhere, it crushed the clouds.

> [1] monsoon – rainy season near the Indian Ocean
> [2] muezzin – a Muslim crier who calls people to prayer from a mosque
> [3] ululating – wailing
> [4] dais – low platform

Reading tip 📖

Using words and phrases such as 'perhaps' 'maybe' or 'it's possible that' suggest you are interpreting the text and raising interesting ideas of your own.

In this text there is **explicit** information, such as the fact that Nazneen waits before she crosses the road. There are also **implicit** ideas that we understand without being told, for example, that Nazneen is nervous and uncertain about how to cross the road.

As readers, we can **interpret** ideas from the text, which means we can explain the meaning behind the ideas. One interpretation would be that Nazneen may not have experienced traffic like this before in her village in Bangladesh.

Key terms 🔑

Explicit: clearly stated, you just need to find it

Implicit: suggested; you have to interpret the text to work it out for yourself

Interpret: explain the meaning of something in your own words, showing your understanding

Activity ①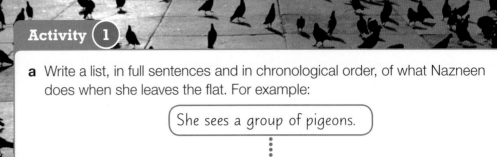

a Write a list, in full sentences and in chronological order, of what Nazneen does when she leaves the flat. For example:

> She sees a group of pigeons.

↓

> She sees a woman carrying a crying child.

b Imagine you are Nazneen. Using your list, add thought bubbles to each item. They should reflect your interpretation of Nazneen's reactions to what she sees and how she feels. For example:

She sees a group of pigeons.

> They seem tired and imprisoned. I feel like that a bit after my journey to this strange place.

She sees a woman carrying a crying child.

> The child seems upset as though she is a prisoner of the woman. I also feel like a prisoner in this threatening place.

When you are analysing a reading text, you need to use *quotations*. They support the points you make about implicit meanings.

For each idea you identify and interpret, you need to use a quotation from the text. For example:

> Nazneen sees a woman carrying a screaming child. She calls her 'the kidnapper' which suggests that Nazneen is unsure if the woman is really the child's mother. Perhaps Nazneen herself feels that this place is threatening and this makes her see things negatively.

Activity (2)

Explain what you understand about Nazneen's first experience of the city.
Use quotations to support your answer.

2 The city of London

Skills and objectives

- To analyse how writers use language and structure to create effects **(AO2)**
- To evaluate how effective writers are at creating character and settings through language **(AO4)**

Key term 🔑

Personification: giving something human qualities, as if it is a person

One writer who has been obsessed about the city of London in his writing is the novelist Peter Ackroyd. He has even written a non-fiction book called *London: a biography* as if the city is a living, breathing person.

Read the extract from a newspaper interview with Peter Ackroyd below. Notice how he describes London using **personification.**

Extract from the *Guardian* website, August 2003

Tales of the City

Yet London is his great love. Virtually all his books, whether biographies of Dickens or Blake, or novels such as *Hawksmoor* and *Dan Leno and the Limehouse Golem*, have been, in one way or another, about London. How would he describe the character of
5 London? "Well, I think it's male, a great age, unpredictable, it's diseased, it's impatient, it's energetic... that's it."
 Is the character of London close to his own? "No. No, I don't think so." Describe your own character, I say. "It's male, it's old,
10 it's diseased, it's impatient. I don't know, that's it." It sounds pretty close to London, I say. "Does it really? Noooooooah. No similarities at all."

Activity 1

a Look carefully at the notes made below in the spider diagram about Ackroyd's London.

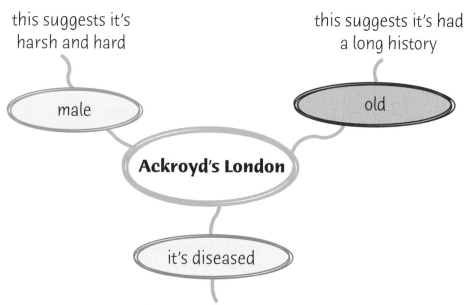

this suggests it's harsh and hard

this suggests it's had a long history

male

old

Ackroyd's London

it's diseased

perhaps this implies that the city has a dark side, for example with crime or greed for money since so much business is there

b Think about a city, town or village that you know well, perhaps where you or a family member lives, or a place you visit in the holidays.

c Jot down some notes as a spider diagram about how you would characterize it. If you had to personify it, as Ackroyd does with London, what would its characteristics be? Use some of the questions below to help you.

– If it was a colour, what would it be?

– If it was a gender, which would it be?

– If it was an age, what would that be?

– If it was an emotion, what would it be?

– If it was a taste, what would it be?

– If it was an object, what would it be?

d Discuss your chosen place with a partner and explain its characteristics.

Now read a description of the dark side of London from Peter Ackroyd's novel *Hawksmoor*. Ackroyd uses his descriptions of the London streets as a chilling setting for murder and mystery. He sets up two parallel stories. The first is about Nicholas Dyer, who builds seven churches in 18th-century London which he uses for secret, evil human sacrifices. The second story is about Nicholas Hawksmoor, a detective in the 1980s, investigating modern murders committed in the same churches.

Extract from *Hawksmoor* by Peter Ackroyd

And as the cry faded away, the noise of the traffic returned with increased clarity. The group of vagrants were standing in a corner of some derelict ground, where unwanted objects from the city had over the years been deposited: broken bottles and unrecognizable pieces of
5 metal were strewn over a wide area, crab grass[1] and different varieties of tall ragweed[1] partially obscured the shapes of abandoned or burnt-out cars, while rotting mattresses sank into the soil. A hoarding[2] had been erected by the river side: it was of a dark red colour, but from here the images were indistinct and only the words HAVE ANOTHER
10 BEFORE YOU GO were still visible. Now, in the early summer, this forgotten area had the sweet, rank, dizzying odour of decay. The vagrants had started a fire, piling up the old rags and newspapers which they found lying beside them, and were now dancing around it – or, rather, they stumbled backwards and forwards with their fire as
15 the wavering centre. They shouted out words in the air but they were too deeply imbued[3] in alcohol or meths[4] to know either the time or the place in which they found themselves. A light rain fell across their faces as they stared upward from the turning earth.

Some distance away from them, in a corner of the ground closest
20 to the Thames, a solitary tramp was staring at the figure in the dark coat who was now walking away: 'Do you remember me?' the tramp cried out, 'You're the one, aren't you! I've seen you! I've watched you!' The figure paused for a moment before hurrying on; then the tramp's attention shifted and, forgetting all about the man (who had even now
25 reached the river and stood with his back towards the city), he bent over once more and continued digging with his hands into the damp earth. Behind him the outline of the Limehouse church could be seen against the darkening sky; he gazed up at the building, with its massive but now crumbling and discoloured stone, and rubbed his neck with
30 the palm of his right hand. 'It's getting cold,' he said, 'I'm off. I've had enough of this. I'm cold.'

[1]crab grass and ragweed – wild plants/weeds
[2]hoarding – large board for advertising
[3]imbued – filled
[4]meths – methylated spirit (a type of alcoholic liquid, not supposed to be drunk)

Activity 2

What is the effect of the writer's choice of descriptive words and phrases? Explore the **connotations** of the words used and what they suggest about the setting of this novel.

> 'group of vagrants'

> 'derelict ground'

> 'rotting mattresses'

> 'sweet, rank, dizzying odour of decay'

> 'the images were indistinct'

Use some of the sentence starters below to help you structure your answers.

- The word... suggests...
- The phrase... gives the impression...
- The choice of the word... conveys the idea...
- Ackroyd's use of the word....
- The word... makes me think...
- The connotations of the word... are... This suggests London is...

Activity 3

This extract names features of this setting using **proper nouns** and **common nouns**. The writer describes two slightly separate areas: the first is where the group of vagrants stand; the second area is where a lone tramp watches.

a Draw a diagram of the setting and label the ten features that you consider most important, using nouns that the author himself has chosen.

b The writer structures his writing using separate paragraphs about the two separate areas. The first paragraph shows a bleak group of vagrants. The **mood** becomes even darker in the second paragraph.

- What is the topic of the second paragraph?
- Pick out three phrases that convey loneliness and threat. Explain why you have chosen them.

Activity 4

Using your responses to the activities above, answer the following question in two paragraphs using quotations:

> How does the writer use language and structure to create setting and atmosphere in this extract?

Key terms

Connotation: an idea or feeling suggested by a word, in addition to the main meaning. For example, the connotations of the word 'beach' might be sunshine or gritty sand, depending on your experience of the beach

Proper noun: a word that names a particular place or person. They always start with a capital letter

Common noun: a common noun identifies a person, place or thing, but does not need a capital letter)

Mood: the feeling or atmosphere conveyed by a piece of writing

3 Rambling into danger

Skills and objectives

- To analyse how writers use structure to influence readers **(AO2)**
- To evaluate how effective writers are at presenting characters **(AO4)**

The writer below has chosen a very different setting for his novel. The following extract from the opening chapter of Ross Raisin's contemporary novel *God's Own Country* takes place on the Yorkshire Moors.

Extract from *God's Own Country* by Ross Raisin

Ramblers. Daft sods in pink hats and green hats. It wasn't even cold. They moved down the field swing-swaying like a line of drunks, addled[1] with the air and the land, and the smell of manure. I watched them from up top, their bright heads peeping through the fog.

5 Sat on my rock there I let the world busy itself below, all manner of creatures going about their backwards-forwards same as always, never mind the fog had them half-sighted. But I could see above the fog. It bided[2] under my feet, settled in the valley like a sump-pool[3] spreading three miles over to the hills at Felton.

10 The ramblers hadn't marked[4] me. They'd walked past the farm without taking any notice, of me or of Father rounding up the flock from the moor. Oi there ramblers, I'd a mind for shouting, what the bugger are you doing, talking to that sheep? Do you think she fancies a natter, eh? And they'd have bowed down royal for me then, no doubt. So sorry,
15 Mr Farmer, we won't do it again, I hope we haven't upset her. For that was the way with these – so respect-minded they wouldn't dare even look on myself for fear of crapping up Nature's balance. The laws of the countryside. And me, I was real, living, farting Nature to their brain of things, part of the scenery same as a tree or a tractor. I watched as the
20 last one over the stile fiddled with a rock on top the wall, for he thought he'd knocked it out of place weighting himself over. Daft sods these ramblers. I went towards them.

Halfway down the field the fog got hold of me, feeling around my face so as I had to stop a minute and tune my eyes, though I still had sight
25 of the hats, no bother. They were only a short way into the next field, moving on like a line of chickens, their heads twitching side to side. What a lovely molehill. Look Bob, a cuckoo behind the drystone wall[5]. Only it wasn't a cuckoo, I knew, it was a bloody pigeon.

[1]addled – confused
[2]bided – stayed
[3]sump-pool – a basin in which water collects
[4]marked – noticed
[5]drystone wall – wall made from stone without any mortar (to stick it together)

The main character in this story is the narrator, Sam Marsdyke. The reader learns a lot about Sam from what he says, does and thinks.

Key term 🔑

Summarize: to give the main points of something briefly

Activity 1

Answer the following questions, using quotations to support your ideas:

- How old do you think Sam is?
- What job does Sam do?
- How does Sam react to the ramblers?
- What do you understand about how Sam feels about the countryside?
- Find examples of Sam's use of slang and informal language in this extract?
- **Summarize** how Sam thinks the ramblers feel about the countryside.

Structure is the way a writer organizes the text. Writers use a range of structural features to influence readers. The words and phrases in italics below are useful terms to use when writing about structure.

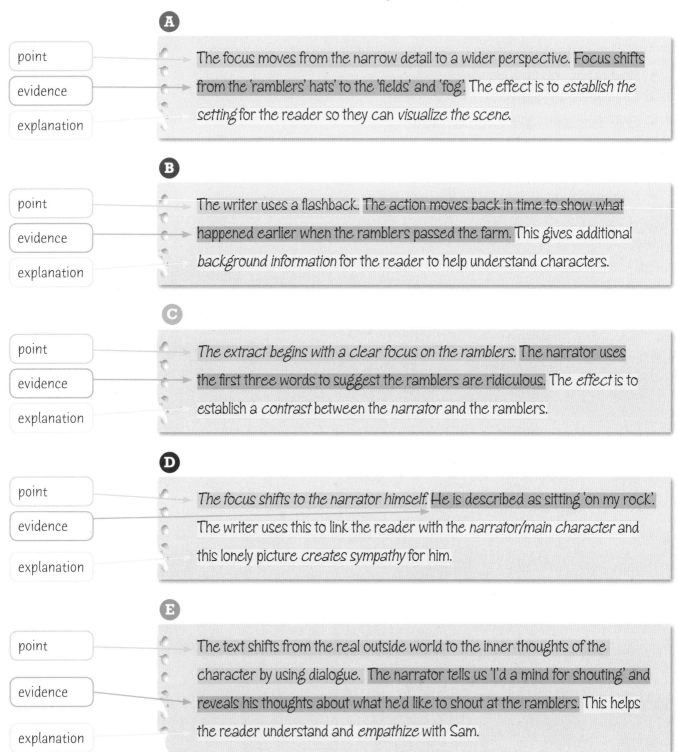

A

point
evidence
explanation

The focus moves from the narrow detail to a wider perspective. Focus shifts from the 'ramblers' hats' to the 'fields' and 'fog'. The effect is to *establish the setting* for the reader so they can *visualize the scene*.

B

point
evidence
explanation

The writer uses a flashback. The action moves back in time to show what happened earlier when the ramblers passed the farm. This gives additional *background information* for the reader to help understand characters.

C

point
evidence
explanation

The extract begins with a clear focus on the ramblers. The narrator uses the first three words to suggest the ramblers are ridiculous. The *effect* is to establish a *contrast* between the *narrator* and the ramblers.

D

point
evidence
explanation

The focus shifts to the narrator himself. He is described as sitting 'on my rock'. The writer uses this to link the reader with the *narrator/main character* and this lonely picture *creates sympathy* for him.

E

point
evidence
explanation

The text shifts from the real outside world to the inner thoughts of the character by using dialogue. The narrator tells us 'I'd a mind for shouting' and reveals his thoughts about what he'd like to shout at the ramblers. This helps the reader understand and *empathize* with Sam.

4 Distant forests

- To explore how writers use language and structure to create effects **(AO2)**
- To write a narrative piece, using a range of structural and linguistic features **(AO5, AO6)**

Below is a complete short story by the writer Angela Carter. She has used a rural setting to create something very different from the peaceful retreat of ramblers. Her tale is a modern adaptation of a famous story. Can you recognize it? She develops the idea of the countryside as a place where secrets can hide and weird ancient practices remain, although the main female character is portrayed as a modern woman.

'The Werewolf' by Angela Carter

It is a northern country; they have cold weather, they have cold hearts.

Cold; tempest; wild beasts in the forest. It is a hard life. Their houses are built of logs, dark and smoky within. There will be a crude icon of the virgin behind a guttering[1] candle, the leg of a pig hung up to cure, a
5 string of drying mushrooms. A bed, a stool, a table. Harsh, brief, poor lives.

To these upland woodsmen, the Devil is as real as you or I. More so; they have not seen us nor even know that we exist, but the Devil they glimpse often in the graveyards, those bleak and touching townships of
10 the dead where the graves are marked with portraits of the deceased in the naif[2] style and there are no flowers to put in front of them, no flowers grow there, so they put out small votive offerings, little loaves, sometimes a cake that the bears come lumbering from the margins of the forests to snatch away. At midnight, especially on Walpurgisnacht[3],
15 the Devil holds picnics in the graveyards and invites the witches; then they dig up fresh corpses, and eat them. Anyone will tell you that.

Wreaths of garlic on the doors keep out the vampires. A blue-eyed child born feet first on the night of St. John's Eve will have second sight. When they discover a witch - some old woman whose cheeses
20 ripen when her neighbours' do not, another old woman whose black cat, oh, sinister! follows her about all the time, they strip the crone, search for her marks, for the supernumerary[4] nipple her familiar[5] sucks. They soon find it. Then they stone her to death.

Winter and cold weather.

25 Go and visit grandmother, who has been sick. Take her the oatcakes I've baked for her on the hearthstone and a little pot of butter.

The good child does as her mother bids - five miles' trudge through the forest; do not leave the path because of the bears, the wild boar, the starving wolves. Here, take your father's hunting knife; you know how
30 to use it.

The child had a scabby coat of sheepskin to keep out the cold, she knew the forest too well to fear it but she must always be on her guard. When she heard that freezing howl of a wolf, she dropped her gifts, seized
35 her knife, and turned on the beast.

It was a huge one, with red eyes and running, grizzled chops; any but a mountaineer's child would have died of fright at the sight of it. It went for her throat, as wolves do, but she made a great swipe at it with her father's
40 knife and slashed off its right forepaw.

The wolf let out a gulp, almost a sob, when it saw what had happened to it; wolves are less brave than they seem. It went lolloping off disconsolately[6] between the trees as well as it could on three legs, leaving a trail of blood
45 behind it. The child wiped the blade of her knife clean on her apron, wrapped up the wolf's paw in the cloth in which her mother had packed the oatcakes and went on towards her grandmother's house. Soon it came on to snow so thickly that the path and any footsteps, track or spoor that might have been upon it were obscured.

50 She found her grandmother was so sick she had taken to her bed and fallen into a fretful sleep, moaning and shaking so that the child guessed she had a fever. She felt the forehead, it burned. She shook out the cloth from her basket, to use it to make the old woman a cold compress, and the wolf's paw fell to the floor.

55 But it was no longer a wolf's paw. It was a hand, chopped off at the wrist, a hand toughened with work and freckled with old age. There was a wedding ring on the third finger and a wart in the index finger. By the wart, she knew it for her grandmother's hand.

She pulled back the sheet but the old woman woke up, at that, and began to
60 struggle, squawking and shrieking like a thing possessed. But the child was strong, and armed with her father's hunting knife; she managed to hold her grandmother down long enough to see the cause of her fever. There was a bloody stump where her right hand should have been, festering already.

The child crossed herself and cried out so loud the neighbours heard her and
65 come rushing in. They know the wart on the hand at once for a witch's nipple; they drove the old woman, in her shift as she was, out into the snow with sticks, beating her old carcass as far as the edge of the forest, and pelted her with stones until she fell dead.

Now the child lived in her grandmother's house; she prospered.

[1]guttering – burning unsteadily
[2]naif – simple
[3]Walpurgisnacht – Witches Night
[4]supernumerary – extra
[5]familiar – demon
[6]disconsolately – unhappily

In the previous section (pages 152–154), you saw how the writer structured an extract by starting from a *detailed view* of the characters, then *broadening that view* to take in a *wider perspective* of the landscape. Here, Carter does the reverse. She begins with the setting and then focuses in on the individual to convey a modern view of how the story should portray the girl. The tale ends with a surprising twist.

Activity 1

With a partner discuss the following:

- Which aspects of the story's setting suggest it is set in the countryside and in an isolated countryside area?
- Which aspects feel modern and different from the traditional version of this story that you know?
- What is your personal reaction to this story? Did you enjoy it? What did you find interesting?

The writer's language is evocative and atmospheric. She uses words which create a very particular setting and mood.

Key term

Theme: a central idea running through a text, often reflected by patterns of words that are linked to it, for example, love, violence, nature

Activity 2

Carter develops her ideas through the use of **themes** that weave through her story.

a Copy and complete the box below with examples of words that develop these themes in this story. An example is done for you.

b Use the sixth box to identify your own category and give examples.

The supernatural	Superstitions	The family
Animals and nature	Family Grandmother Good girl Mother Wedding ring Father	[your idea]

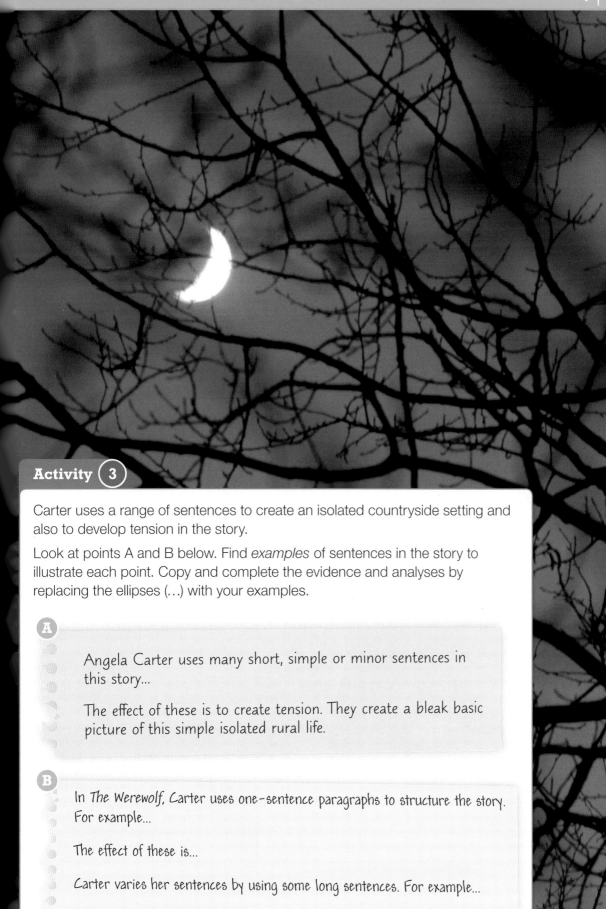

Activity ③

Carter uses a range of sentences to create an isolated countryside setting and also to develop tension in the story.

Look at points A and B below. Find *examples* of sentences in the story to illustrate each point. Copy and complete the evidence and analyses by replacing the ellipses (…) with your examples.

A

> Angela Carter uses many short, simple or minor sentences in this story...
>
> The effect of these is to create tension. They create a bleak basic picture of this simple isolated rural life.

B

> In *The Werewolf*, Carter uses one-sentence paragraphs to structure the story. For example...
>
> The effect of these is...
>
> Carter varies her sentences by using some long sentences. For example...
>
> For the reader, these create...

You have seen how Carter uses language, themes and sentence structures to create the setting for an unsettling tale. Now you will write a short narrative of your own where the setting has an effect on the action. Use her story as a model.

Activity 4

a Look at the two images on pages 160–161 below. Think of a city setting where you can write about an unsettling series of events.

b How we regard what is happening depends on our point of view. Some might see them as positive and exciting. Others might see them as a reflection of greed and emptiness. With a partner consider the following:

- What aspects of city life are reflected in these pictures?
- What could be unpleasant about the setting?
- What, in terms of people and their behaviour, could be seen as strange?
- What events might happen in these settings that you could base a story upon?

Activity 5

a Choose one of the two pictures as the starting point for your story. Plan your story. You will need to consider the following to help you.

- Setting – how you will describe the city to make it unsettling. (Carter mentions items that reflect superstition and isolation.)

- Characters – think about how you can emphasize the city as an anonymous and lonely place. (Carter does not give her characters names.)

- Language – consider how you can vary sentences to create mood and pace. (Carter uses short sentences at the beginning of her story.)

- Structure – how you will direct the focus of the reader and organize your ideas. Make sure you plan the focus of each paragraph.

b Write two sentences that might open a piece of writing about the image of your choice – using Carter's story as a model.

Activity 6

Write your story in full. When it is complete, proofread your work, checking your spelling and punctuation.

Writing tip

Remember the main reasons why you would start a new paragraph:

- Shift in time
- Shift in place
- Shift in topic
- Shift in perspective: this shows the reader that the focus has moved from one character's actions, point of view or speech to another's.

5 Sounds of the city

Skills and objectives

- To summarize and compare writers' ideas, with reference to the language they use **(AO3)**

- To write clearly and organize ideas **(AO5)**

Cities are busy places, full of people, activity, traffic and noise. This is nothing new, according to a journalist's account of spring in the city written in New York, in 1871.

Extract from 'Budding Spring – In the City' written by F. Fern.

We of the city do not appreciate the blessing of closed windows and silence, until budding Spring comes. The terrific war-whoop[1] of the milkman inaugurates[2] the new-born day long before we should otherwise recognize it. Following him is the rag-man, with his handcart,
5 to which six huge jangling, terrific cow-bells are fastened, as an accompaniment to the yet louder yell of 'r-a-g-s'. Then comes the 'S-t-r-a-w-b-e-r-r-y' man, with lungs of leather, splitting your head, as you try to sip your coffee in peace. Close upon his heels, before he has hardly turned the corner, comes the pine-apple man, who tries to
10 outscreech *him*. Then the fish-man, who blows a hideous tin trumpet, loud enough and discordant[3] enough to set all your nerves jangling, if they had not already been taxed to the utmost.

You jump up in a frenzy to close the window, only to see that the fish-man has stopped his abominable cart at the door of a neighbor,
15 where he is deliberately cleaning and splitting them, and throwing the refuse[4] matter in the street, as a bouquet for your nostrils during the warm day. […] By this time comes a great mob of boys, with vigorous lungs, tossing each other's caps in the air, and screeching with a power perfectly inexplicable at only six, ten, or twelve years of practice. Indeed,
20 the smaller the boy the bigger is his war-whoop, as a general rule. […]

By this time your hair stands on end, and beads of perspiration form upon your nose. You fly for refuge[5] to the back of the house. Alas! In the next house is a little dog barking as if his last hour was coming; while upon the shed are two cats, in the most inflamed[6] state of bristle,
25 glaring like fiends[7] and '*maow*'-ing in the most hellish manner at each other's whiskers. You go down into the parlor, and seat yourself there. Your neighbour, Tom Snooks, is smoking at his window, and puffing it right through yours over your lovely roses, the perfume of which he quite extinguishes with his nasty odor.

30 Heavens! And this is 'Spring'!

[1]war-whoop – a battle cry
[2]inaugurates – introduces
[3]discordant – harsh sounding
[4]refuse – rubbish
[5]refuge – safety
[6]inflamed – angry
[7]fiends - devils

The journalist presents a clear perspective in this article: the city is noisy. Think carefully about her point of view:

Is she merely observing, does she like the sounds or does she hate them?

a Copy the emotion chart below and mark the writer's point of view about the city on it.

1	2	3	4	5	6	7	8	9	10
Extremely negative				Objective			Extremely positive		

b Write three lines, using quotations, explaining your choice.

There are more details about this point of view which you need to be able to identify and support with quotations.

Activity 2

Find a quotation from the extract to support the following statements:

a The milkman arrives early in the morning.

b The rag-man's bells are noisy.

c The journalist wants peace and quiet.

d It is not only the noise which is annoying.

To identify the writer's perspective, read the article carefully. After every sentence, ask yourself, 'What point is the writer making here? Is this the same point or a new one?'

Don't just copy out (restate) the point the writer makes. You need to identify what the writer *thinks* or *feels* about their topic. For example:

Omar

The writer *goes to the back of the house because of all the noise at the front of the house. There is a dog barking, cats screeching and a man is 'smoking at his window'.*

Finley

The writer tries to escape from the noise by saying 'fly for refuge' which shows how desperate the writer is, but there is a dog barking and cats screeching in the garden too. The word 'Alas!' shows the writer's surprise and distress at not finding any peace there either.

Activity 3

a Which student has simply restated what the writer has said?

b Which student has commented on the writer's viewpoint by explaining how the writer feels about it?

Activity 4

Analyse how the writer uses language.

a Link each descriptive phrase with what they describe in the text.

a) 'terrific war-whoop'	1) the rubbish thrown out in the street
b) 'a bouquet for your nostrils'	2) the milkman's shouting
c) 'fly for refuge'	3) the speaker herself

b Pick the best words from those presented in italics for the analysis below.

In 'Budding Spring' the writer describes the noises of the city as *exciting/unbearable/relaxing*. The busy city is conveyed by her use of lists such as the procession of rag-man, strawberry man, pineapple man and fish man. The words she chooses to convey her viewpoint suggest that she is a *relaxed/anxious/lonely* person. She uses *exaggeration/understatement/facts* to convey her viewpoint to the reader.

A second article, written in 2010, offers a very different perspective on sound in the city.

Extract from the *Guardian* by Amelia Hill, 2010

Why we love sounds of the city jungle

For some, living in a city is a loud, unpleasant babble of intrusive[1] noise. For others it is a soundscape of calming tones that lift the spirits and brighten the day. Now a £1m research project is building a database of noises that people say improve their environment. It
5 will translate those findings into design principles to help architects create sweeter-sounding cities.

Among the urban sounds researchers have found to be surprisingly agreeable are car tyres on wet, bumpy asphalt[2], the distant roar of a motorway flyover, the rumble of an overground
10 train and the thud of heavy bass heard on the street outside a nightclub.

Other sounds that are apparently kind to the ear include a baby laughing, skateboarders practising in underground car parks and orchestras tuning up.

15 'Sound in the environment, especially that made by other people, has overwhelmingly been considered purely as a matter of volume and generally in negative terms, as both intrusive and undesirable,' said Dr Bill Davies of Salford University, who is leading […] the project Positive
20 Soundscapes. […]

According to the latest National Noise Incidence Study, moves to bring in quieter transport and urban noise barriers are falling short. Traffic noise is audible in 87 per cent of homes in England and
25 Wales, and 54 per cent of the population is exposed to levels beyond the World Health Organisation guidelines for avoiding serious irritation.

Davies would like to see more water features and sound-generating sculptures next to busy
30 roads. Buildings and trees can also be used to scatter, deaden or reflect sound, to create peaceful, quieter spaces or vibrant[3], exciting-sounding areas. […]

Sounds are not, the study found, judged solely
35 on volume. 'The frequency [pitch] of a noise is a huge issue,' said Davies. 'A high-pitched sound is unpleasant even if it is very quiet, like the whine of a wasp trapped in a room, while a sound like bass coming through the wall of a nightclub, which is loud but low, can be very soothing.'

[1]intrusive – unwanted
[2]asphalt – road covering
[3]vibrant – lively

Activity 5

Write a summary of the differences between the sounds of the city in 1871 and in 2010.

To do this, use a table to list of all the sounds described in the first article on page 162. Do the same for the second article on page 166. Do any of these sounds appear in both articles? Use your lists to answer the question.

Sound	1871	2010
tradesmen, for example, milkmen		

Activity 6

What does each of these quotations tell you about the writer's perspective in the second text?

a 'For some… For others…'

b 'surprisingly agreeable'

c 'both intrusive and undesirable'

d 'to create peaceful, quieter spaces or vibrant, exciting-sounding areas'

e 'can be very soothing'

When comparing writers' perspectives, you need to identify *what* those perspectives are, as well as comparing *how* they present them to the reader. In this question you will focus particularly on language and tone.

You must plan your comparison. Your plan might look like this:

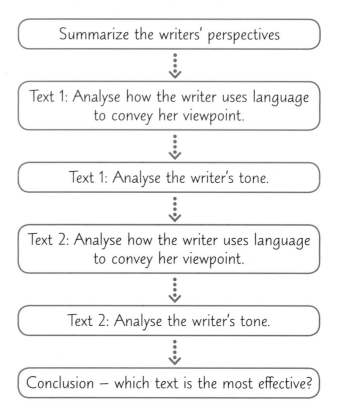

Summarize the writers' perspectives

Text 1: Analyse how the writer uses language to convey her viewpoint.

Text 1: Analyse the writer's tone.

Text 2: Analyse how the writer uses language to convey her viewpoint.

Text 2: Analyse the writer's tone.

Conclusion – which text is the most effective?

Or like this:

	Text 1	Text 2	Both texts
1 Introduction – summarize the writers' perspectives			X
2 Analyse how the writer uses language to convey her viewpoint	X		
3 Analyse writer's tone	X		
4 Analyse how the writer uses language to convey her viewpoint		X	
5 Analyse writer's tone		X	
6 Conclusion – which text is the most effective?			X

Activity 7

Compare how attitudes to city sounds are presented differently in the two texts.

Plan your answer first, using one of the models above and use quotations to support your points.

Using your work from Activity 7, you are now going to write an article to present your *own* perspective on noise in the modern world.

- Use what you have learned about descriptive language and tone from the two texts you have read.
- Aim to write an introduction, at least two paragraphs (one about each text) and a conclusion.
- Plan the focus of each paragraph before you start writing.

Activity 8

'Peace is a luxury of the past. There is no escape from the horror of noise in the modern world.'

Write an article arguing your point of view about noise in the modern world. You might agree, disagree or give a mixed view about the above statement.

Progress check

In this chapter you have developed some key skills. Complete the progress check below to see how confident you now feel about applying these skills.

Key skills	Confident I understand how to do this.	OK Sometimes I understand how to do this.	Not sure I need to practise this more.
I can identify and interpret explicit and implicit ideas.			
I can select and summarize evidence from texts.			
I can analyse how writers use language and structure to create effects.			
I can compare writers' ideas and how they present ideas across different texts.			
I can evaluate how successful writers have been.			
I can write for different purposes, choosing the right tone and style.			
I can organize my ideas and use structural features to communicate clearly.			

Assessment

This section tests all the reading and writing skills that you have learned in this chapter to see if you are able to apply them to different texts.

Read the extract below and complete the activities that follow. The extract is taken from an account of a country childhood, written in 1959, called *Cider with Rosie*.

Extracts from *Cider with Rosie* by Laurie Lee

Walking downstairs there was a smell of floorboards, of rags, sour lemons, old spices. The smoky kitchen was in its morning muddle, from which breakfast would presently emerge. Mother stirred the porridge,
5 in a soot-black pot. Tony was carving bread with a ruler, the girls in their mackintoshes were laying the table, and the cats were eating the butter. I cleaned some boots and pumped up some fresh water; Jack went for a jug of skimmed milk.

10 'I'm all behind,' Mother said to the fire. 'This wretched coal's all slack.'

She snatched up an oil-can and threw it all on the fire. A belch of flame roared up the chimney. Mother gave a loud scream, as she always did,
15 and went on stirring the porridge.

'If I had a proper stove,' she said. 'It's a trial getting you off each day.'

I sprinkled some sugar on a slice of bread and bolted it down while I could. How different again
20 looked the kitchen this morning, swirling with smoke and sunlight. Some cut-glass vases threw jagged rainbows across the piano's field of dust, while Father in his pince-nez[1] up on the wall looked down like a scandalized god.

25 At last the porridge was dabbed on our plates from a thick and steaming spoon. I covered the smoky lumps with treacle and began to eat from the sides to the middle. The girls round the table chewed moonishly[2], wrapped in their morning stupor. Still
30 sick with sleep, their mouths moved slow, hung

slack while their spoon came up; then they paused for a moment, spoon to lip, collected their wits, and ate. Their vacant eyes stared straight before them, glazed at the sight of the day. Pink and glowing from their dreamy beds, from who knows what arms of 35 heroes, they seemed like mute[3] spirits hauled back to the earth after paradise feasts of love.

'Golly!' cried Doth. 'Have you seen the time?'

They began to jump to their feet.

'Goodness, it's late.' 40

'I got to be off.'

'Me too.'

'Lord, where's my things?'

'Well, ta-ta Ma; ta boys – be good.'

***

But what should we boys do, now they had all 45 gone? If it was school-time, we pushed off next. If not, we dodged up the bank to play, ran snail races along the walls, or dug in the garden and found potatoes and cooked them in tins on the rubbish heap. We were always hungry, always calling for 50 food, always seeking it in cupboards and hedges. But holiday times were a time of risk, there might be housework or errands to do. Mother would be ironing, or tidying-up, or reading books on the floor. So if we hung around the yard we kept our ears 55 cocked; if she caught us, the game was up.

[1]pince-nez – glasses with a nose clip rather than earpieces
[2]moonishly – dreamily
[3]mute – silent

This activity will secure your knowledge about **how to select and interpret ideas (AO1)**.

Activity 1

a List four things the writer does in the morning.

b What do you learn from the extract about the writer's family?

c What do you learn about the kitchen?

d How do you think the writer feels about his childhood home?

This activity will secure your knowledge about **how writers use language to create effects (A02)**.

Activity 2

a Explore how the writer uses lists in the extract to create effects.

b What is the effect of the description of his father's picture on the wall?

c Why do you think the writer describes his sisters as 'chewing moonishly'?

d Using your answers to the above, and any other examples of language that you find effective, answer the following question:

How does the writer use language to create a vivid impression of family life?

This activity will secure your knowledge about **how writers use text structure for particular purposes (A02)**.

Activity 3

a Look carefully at the two sections of *Cider with Rosie* on page 170.

  • What is the focus of the first section (up to 'be good')?

  • What is the focus of the second section from 'But what should we boys do' to the end?

b Look at the fifth paragraph, as the writer reflects on his surroundings. What does it reveal about his feelings about his home?

c Why do you think the writer chooses to include dialogue in this description?

d What is the effect of using a first-person narrative in this extract?

This activity will secure your knowledge of **how to evaluate writing using references to the text (AO4)**. Note that in the exam, this skill will be applied to a fiction text, but the same skill can also be applied to non-fiction texts.

Activity 4

a Some of the writer's descriptions are amusing. Find examples of this in the extract and explain their effect on the reader.

b How successful has the writer been in presenting the character of his mother?

c Using what you have learned about language, structure and tone, evaluate how effective you think the writer is in capturing the reader's interest in his memories of childhood.

The following extract is taken from *Mrs Beeton's Book of Household Management*, which was first published in 1861. This extract gives guidance to women on how they should run their households.

Extract from *Mrs Beeton's Book of Household Management* by Isabella Beeton

HAVING THUS INDICATED some of the more general duties of the mistress, [...] we will now give a few specific instructions on matters having a more practical relation to the position which she is supposed to occupy in the eye of the world. To do this the more clearly, we will
5 begin with her earliest duties, and take her completely through the occupations of a day.

HAVING RISEN EARLY, [...] and having given due attention to the bath, and made a careful toilet, it will be well at once to see that the children have received their proper ablutions[1], and are in every way clean and
10 comfortable. The first meal of the day, breakfast, will then be served, at which all the family should be punctually present, unless illness, or other circumstances, prevent.

AFTER BREAKFAST IS OVER, it will be well for the mistress to make a round of the kitchen and other offices, to see that all are in order, and
15 that the morning's work has been properly performed by the various domestics[2]. The orders for the day should then be given, and any questions which the domestics desire to ask, respecting their several departments, should be answered, and any special articles they may require, handed to them from the store-closet.

20 In those establishments where there is a housekeeper, it will not be so necessary for the mistress, personally, to perform the above-named duties.

AFTER THIS GENERAL SUPERINTENDENCE[3] of her servants, the mistress, if a mother of a young family, may devote herself to the
25 instruction of some of its younger members, or to the examination of the state of their wardrobe[4], leaving the later portion of the morning for reading, or for some amusing recreation[5].

[1]ablutions – washing
[2]domestics – servants
[3]superintendence – checking
[4]wardrobe – clothing
[5]recreation – leisure activity

Both of these texts give the reader a perspective on family life.

This activity will secure your knowledge of **how to summarize evidence from different texts (AO1)**.

Activity 5

Using quotations from both texts, summarize the similarities and differences between the role of the mother, as described in the extracts.

This activity will secure your knowledge of **how to compare writers' points of view (AO3)**.

Activity 6

Compare how the two texts present a different perspective on family life.
You should consider:

- the writers' viewpoints
- language
- structure
- tone.

This activity will secure your knowledge of **how to write clearly and effectively, organizing your ideas in a clear structure and using appropriate and accurate language (AO5, AO6)**.

Activity 7

Write the text for a booklet for modern parents, providing guidance on the challenges of managing a modern household and family. You might want to use some of the following headings for sections:

- Essential and non-essential household tasks
- Sharing domestic duties among the family
- Managing household duties as well as a job
- Bringing up young children or teenagers
- Food: shopping and cooking
- Cleaning
- Creating a happy household
- Money management.

6 Revisiting the Assessment Objectives

So far in this book you have read extracts of writing from different genres and different centuries, and you have learned and practised a number of reading and writing skills.

This chapter is different. It looks ahead to next year when you will apply these skills to your GCSE English Language examination. You will sit two different papers and your work will be marked according to Assessment Objectives.

This chapter revisits each of the Assessment Objectives in turn. It shows you exactly *where*, *when* and *how* to apply the necessary skills. The activities will revise the relevant skills and prepare you for any internal exams at this mid-point in the course.

Assessment Objective 1 (AO1)

Read and understand a range of texts to:
- identify and interpret explicit and implicit information and ideas
- select and synthesize evidence from different texts.

In simple terms this means:
- understand obvious and underlying ideas in a text
- take information from two texts and combine them.

Where is AO1 tested in the exam?
- Paper 1, Question 1
- Paper 2, Question 1 and 2

These AO1 skills are very important. You need to master them before you can start to analyse language or structure, evaluate or compare texts.

In the following newspaper article, Tony Parsons offers his views on the subject of tattoos.

Making my skin crawl: Tattoos scream for attention

As soon as the sun starts shining, I realise with a sinking heart that Britain is now a tattooed nation.

Tattoos are everywhere. You see them on firm young flesh and on wobbly, middle-aged flab, as common now
5 on the school run and in the supermarket queue as they are on some footballer or his wife.

I feel like the last man left alive whose skin crawls at the sight of these crass daubings¹. I feel like the only person in the world who sees David Beckham modelling
10 his swimming pants on the cover of *Elle* magazine and thinks – oh, how much better a handsome guy like you would look, David, without all those dumb ink stains stitched into your skin. I feel like nobody else looks at little Cheryl Cole – so pretty, so smiley – and recoils
15 at the sight of the florist shop she has permanently engraved on her lovely body.

[…] Tattoos scream for attention. Tattoos say – look at me! I guess the person with the tattoo imagines that – somehow – having a martial arts symbol or a badly
20 drawn flower or a sentimental heart expresses their individuality. The end result is a million simple souls all with exactly the same primitive² daubings, all telling you what an individual they are.

On Tuesday, a tattooed lady called Joanna Southgate
25 – pretty, blonde, young – swerved past the dress code at Royal Ascot by waiting until she was inside before revealing that her arms are covered in what looks like a three-year-old's finger paintings. Joanna looked so proud. But why? She has ravaged her natural good looks with what, at best, looks like cartoons done by someone who 30 flunked their art GCSE.

Tattoos were her choice. But tattoos are self-mutilation³. Tattoos are a tragedy. Having tenth-rate art on your body for life is now part of the national fabric.

Did I say that Britain is a tattooed nation? Strike that – 35 Britain is the tattooed nation. […]

Tattoos are so widespread, so ugly and so very, very permanent. You can, in theory, have them removed – but a large chunk of your living flesh will go with it.

The tattooed nation will live to regret this voluntary 40 disfigurement⁴. Already I sense that some of our celebs are covering up – you don't see Cheryl Cole's florist shop nearly as often as you used to. It used to be that you made a mark on your body because you couldn't make a mark on the world. With adored multi-millionaires 45 like Beckham stoking the tattoo craze, that is clearly no longer the case. But some things never change.

A tattoo doesn't make you look like an individual. A tattoo makes you look a thicko. You'll all look silly when you're 60. 50

¹daubings – rough, clumsy pictures
²primitive – basic or simple
³self-mutilation – damaging yourself
⁴disfigurement – spoiled appearance

> **Key term** 🔑
>
> **Explicit:** clearly stated; you just need to find it

For AO1, you must identify **explicit** information, which means you need to find it in the text.

> ## Activity (1)
>
> Read again lines 1 to 6. List *four* things from this part of the text about the type of people who wear tattoos.

Also for AO1, you need to look beneath the surface to identify **implicit** information.

> ## Activity (2)
>
> Read again lines 7 to 16. Choose four statements below that are true.
> - The writer dislikes tattoos.
> - The writer thinks that everyone has the same attitude as him regarding tattoos.
> - The writer says that David Beckham has appeared on the cover of *The Sunday Times* magazine.
> - The writer feels that David Beckham would look better without tattoos.
> - The writer thinks David Beckham is handsome.
> - The writer believes Cheryl Cole is pretty.
> - Cheryl Cole has tattoos of hearts on her body.
> - Cheryl Cole's tattoos are only temporary.

Another important skill for AO1 is to **interpret** information and ideas. Remember to:

- use your own words
- select supporting quotations to support your points.

> **Key terms** 🔑
>
> **Implicit:** suggested; you have to interpret the text to work it out for yourself
>
> **Interpret:** explain the meaning of something in your own words, showing your understanding
>
> **Synthesize:** to combine information and ideas from different texts

> ## Activity (3)
>
> **a** Read again lines 17 to 23. How is Tony Parsons being humorous when he says: 'The end result is a million simple souls all with exactly the same primitive daubings, all telling you what an individual they are'?
>
> **b** Read again lines 24 to 31.
> - What do the phrases 'pretty, blonde, young', 'looked so proud' and 'ravaged her natural good looks' tell us about Tony Parson's attitude towards Joanna Southgate and her tattoos?
> - What other words and phrases in this paragraph support this view?
>
> **c** Read again from line 32 to the end of the article. What further points does Tony Parsons make to develop his views about tattoos?
>
> **d** Using all the work you have done so far on AO1, write your response to the following:
>
> > What do you understand about Tony Parson's views on the subject of tattoos? Use your own words but also quote from the text to support what you say.

When AO1 is tested in Paper 2, Question 2, you will need to **synthesize** information and ideas in two texts and produce new material in the form of a summary. Remember that you need to interpret and make connections between the information and ideas in both texts.

You have already practised this skill in several chapters in the book. It does not matter which genre or which century your texts are from; the skill you apply is exactly the same.

Read the account 'Tattooed Royalty', which was written in 1898. It is also about tattoos, but this time the attitude towards them is very different.

Tattooed Royalty. Queer Stories of a Queer Craze

When royalty hangs onto a craze, you may be assured that the rest of the exclusive world of wealth and power soon follow in the same path, and annex[1] the peculiarities of the pleasures which have given amusement to their heroes born in the purple. [5]

What wonder, then, that tattooing is just now the popular pastime of the leisured world? For one of the best-known men in high European circles, the Grand Duke Alexis of Russia, is most elaborately tattooed. And Prince and Princess Waldemar [10] of Denmark, […] with many others of royal and distinguished rank, have submitted themselves to the tickling, but painless and rather pleasant, sensation afforded by the improved tattooing needle. […] [15]

The present fancy for being tattooed […] mainly exists among men who have travelled much; while ladies have also taken a strong liking to this form of personal decoration, which, from a woman's point of view, is about as expensive as a dress, but not [20] so costly as good jewellery. […] For the purpose of passing her time in the 'off' season, the lady about town now consents to be pricked by the tattoo artist's operating needle, and to [25] have her forearm or shoulder adorned with perhaps such a mark as this – a serpent holding its tail in its mouth – [30] a symbol representing eternity.

In order to form an idea of the kind of work that is wanted by those who give their patronage[2] to this specific class of fine art, a close examination of these illustrations will assist you. The skill of the tattoo [35] artist, to be realized properly and fairly, must be seen in beautiful colours on a white skin – work which is amazing. The sketches he employs are made in various coloured inks. The great skill is in the faithful reproduction of any symbol or picture desired by [40] the sitter. These designs vary in size from a small fly, or bee, to that of an immense Chinese dragon, occupying the whole space offered by the back or chest, or a huge snake many inches in thickness coiling round the body from the knees to the [45] shoulders.

[1]annex – adopt
[2]patronage – custom, to do business with

Summarize the different views of tattoos in the two texts. Use your own words but also quote from both texts to support what you say.

In particular you could include:

- the type of people who have tattoos
- the types of tattoos that are worn
- the popularity of tattoos
- the quality of the artwork
- the different attitudes towards the idea of tattoos.

Key term

Summarize: give the main points of something briefly

Assessment Objective 2 (AO2)

Explain, comment on and analyse how writers use language and structure to achieve effects and influence readers, using linguistic terminology to support your views.

In simple terms this means that you make points in your own words, using correct terms about:

- the writer's choice of words
- how a text has been built
- how it affects the reader.

Where is AO2 tested in the exam?

- Paper 1, Question 2 and 3
- Paper 2, Question 3

Read the extract on page 179, which is the opening of a short story called 'The Pedestrian', written in 1951 by Ray Bradbury. The main character, Leonard Mead, enjoys an evening stroll. This pastime is forbidden in the year AD 2053 because such simple pleasures have been prohibited by an extreme government with absolute power.

For AO2, you must select appropriate examples from the text on which to comment. Careful choice of quotations is important. For example:

The student makes a clear point.

This is a good choice of quotation.

Look at the detailed comments the student is able to make about it.

> In the opening paragraph, the writer sets the scene by using vivid descriptive language.
> For example 'a misty evening in November'. November has many connotations: it is a clear, crisp time of the year but also notoriously cold and damp. The adjective 'misty' suggests a scene that is beautiful and romantic, but could also hint at danger and the unknown.

Extract from 'The Pedestrian' by Ray Bradbury

To enter out into that silence that was the city at
eight o'clock of a misty evening in November, to
put your feet upon that buckling[1] concrete walk, to
step over grassy seams and make your way, hands
5 in pockets, through the silences, that was what Mr.
Leonard Mead most dearly loved to do. He would
stand upon the corner of an intersection[2] and peer
down long moonlit avenues of sidewalk[3] in four
directions, deciding which way to go, but it really
10 made no difference; he was alone in this world of
A.D. 2053, or as good as alone, and with a final
decision made, a path selected, he would stride
off, sending patterns of frosty air before him like the
smoke of a cigar.

15 Sometimes he would walk for hours and miles
and return only at midnight to his house. And on
his way he would see the cottages and homes
with their dark windows, and it was not unequal to
walking through a graveyard where only the faintest
20 glimmers of firefly[4] light appeared in flickers behind
the windows. Sudden grey phantoms seemed to
manifest[5] upon inner room walls where a curtain
was still undrawn against the night, or there were
whisperings and murmurs where a window in a
25 tomb-like building was still open.

On this particular evening he began his journey in
a westerly direction, toward the hidden sea. There
was a good crystal frost in the air; it cut the nose
and made the lungs blaze like a Christmas tree
30 inside; you could feel the cold light going on and off,
all the branches filled with invisible snow. He listened
to the faint push of his soft shoes through autumn
leaves with satisfaction, and whistled a cold quiet

whistle between his teeth, occasionally picking up a
leaf as he passed, examining its skeletal[6] pattern in 35
the infrequent lamplights as he went on, smelling its
rusty smell.

In ten years of walking by night or day, for
thousands of miles, he had never met another
person walking, not once in all that time. 40

He came to a cloverleaf intersection which stood
silent where two main highways crossed the town.
During the day it was a thunderous surge of cars,
the gas stations open, a great insect rustling and
a ceaseless jockeying[7] for position as the scarab 45
beetles[8], a faint incense[9] puttering from their
exhausts, skimmed homeward to the far directions.
But now these highways, too, were like streams in a
dry season, all stone and bed and moon radiance[10].

He turned back on a side street, circling around 50
toward his home. He was within a block of his
destination when the lone car turned a corner quite
suddenly and flashed a fierce white cone of light upon
him. He stood entranced, not unlike a night moth,
stunned by the illumination, and then drawn toward it. 55

A metallic voice called to him: 'Stand still. Stay
where you are! Don't move!'

[1]buckling – bending
[2]intersection – crossroads
[3]sidewalk – pavement
[4]firefly – insect that glows in the dark
[5]manifest – show
[6]skeletal – like a skeleton
[7]jockeying – shuffling
[8]scarab beetle – symbol of death and regeneration in
Ancient Egypt
[9]incense – spicy smell
[10]radiance – glow

Activity 1

Read again lines 1 to 14. Find a simile in this opening paragraph that creates a
similar effect to 'a misty evening', and explain how this choice of language adds
to your understanding of the setting.

Tip ✓

Focus on particular words to demonstrate that you understand what they suggest.

To enter out into that misty evening in Nov concrete walk, to ste pockets, through the dearly loved to do. H

The words 'misty evening' suggest...'

In your explanations for AO2 you must:

- analyse the writer's choice of language
- explain its effect on the reader.

Activity 2

a Read again lines 15 to 25. In this paragraph, Bradbury confirms our suspicions that the atmosphere is negative by using an **extended metaphor** of death. Write about the connotations and effects of the following words and phrases within the context of the story. The first one has been done for you below:

  i 'it was not unequal to walking through a graveyard'
  ii 'grey phantoms seemed to manifest upon inner room walls'
  iii 'tomb-like building'

> **i** This gives the reader a haunting sense of dread. It is as if the neighbourhood is a final resting place for dead people, and a cold, dark stillness surrounds Leonard Mead as he walks the streets. Everything is silent and every minute sound amplified. The buildings appear architecturally lifeless and the people inside them lacking in humanity. Society seems to be literally and metaphorically decaying around him.

b Read again from line 26 to the end of the extract, and comment on the effects of the writer's use of contrast. Focus in particular on the following:

- hot and cold imagery, such as, 'There was a good crystal frost in the air; it cut the nose and made the lungs blaze like a Christmas tree inside.' What could this suggest about Leonard Mead's place in this society?
- the area by night and by day, such as, 'During the day it was a thunderous surge of cars...'. What do the language choices suggest about Leonard Mead's attitude to this society?
- natural versus unnatural imagery, such as, 'He stood entranced, not unlike a night moth, stunned by the illumination' and 'A metallic voice called to him'.

c Using all the work you have done so far on AO2 and any other examples of language in the text that you find effective, write your response to the following question:

> How does Bradbury's use of language influence our impressions of this futuristic society?

Key terms 🔑

Metaphor: a comparison showing the similarity between two quite different things, stating that one actually is the other

Extended metaphor: a **metaphor** that extends the description using comparison to draw a number of links

AO2 is tested in Paper 1, Question 3. The Question 3 focus is on analysing structure – how a text is built. You must think about structure at three different levels:

- whole text level
- paragraph level
- sentence level.

The structure of the extract from 'The Pedestrian' above follows Leonard Mead's journey through his neighbourhood, but each paragraph shifts the reader's focus.

Activity 3

a How does the whole text structure follow Leonard Mead's journey through his neighbourhood? Which directions does he take and where does he go?

b At which line does the text shift between what is happening in the present and what has happened in the past? What effect does this have on the reader?

c The text is a combination of both external actions and internal thoughts. How does this affect our view of Leonard Mead?

d Why does Bradbury choose to begin his story with a long complex sentence that ends in 'that was what Mr. Leonard Mead most dearly loved to do'? How does this contrast with the sentence forms in the final line of the text, and why?

e What is the significance of the single sentence paragraph in lines 38 to 40? What other key sentences or phrases contribute structurally to the reader's growing nervousness?

f Using your answers to the above and anything else in the story that is relevant, write your response to the following:

> How has Ray Bradbury structured his story to build up to the climax in the final line?

Assessment Objective 3 (AO3)

Compare writers' ideas and perspectives, as well as how these are conveyed, across two or more texts.

In simple terms this means that you must pinpoint similarities in the content and ideas in texts and explain how the writers put these across.

Where is AO3 tested in the exam?
• Paper 2, Question 4

In the newspaper article on page 183, Max Davidson offers his views on the subject of neighbours.

How to get on with the neighbours

by Max Davidson

If ever a statistic leapt out and hit me between the eyes, it was that a million Britons have moved house because of disputes[1] with their neighbours.

This finding, from new research by the insurance company CPP, reveals a worrying trend. If you're living next door to someone, surely it's common sense that you should bend over backwards to get on with them? Why make a mortal enemy out of someone with so much power to irritate you?

But common sense, it seems, has gone out of the window. From fences to barbecues to parking spaces to crying babies, minor nuisances have been allowed to escalate to the point where people have moved out of a neighbourhood, rather than deal with disputes in a grown-up way.

Personally, I have had a very mixed bag of neighbours. Some have become good friends, while others held all-night Abba parties, built dodgy extensions, chucked cigarette-ends over the garden fence and had miniature poodles who bayed like the Hound of the Baskervilles[2]. But I wouldn't have let the most annoying of them drive me from my home. It would have felt like a defeat.

Others seem to be less positive, judging by the CPP research. The live-and-let-live attitudes embedded in English culture are unravelling[3].

If anti-social behaviour is on the rise, so is irritability at the anti-social behaviour of others. People who would once have shrugged at smoke from a bonfire, now get on their high horse and hawk[4] their complaints to the council. Often with disastrous consequences.

There is a lot of pent-up anger behind those twitching net curtains. But in many cases improved communication skills would help defuse[5] tensions with neighbours and prevent feuds spiralling out of control.

'Bad relationships between neighbours reflect the hectic pace of modern life,' says psychologist Dr Rob Yeung. 'People don't have time to build healthy relationships with those living next door. They need to develop the art of empathy[6], and see things from their neighbour's point of view rather than rushing to judgment.'

Fail to empathise, assume your neighbours are beyond the pale because their lifestyles are different from yours, and you get trapped in repetitive loops of behaviour. Every day brings fresh flashpoints and accusations fly like tracer bullets across the garden fence.

Good neighbours breed good neighbours, just as bad neighbours breed bad neighbours. But if you want good neighbours, the best way to get them is to be a good neighbour yourself. A few more smiles on the street wouldn't hurt, would they?

[1]disputes – arguments
[2]Hound of the Baskervilles – legendary supernatural dog featured in a Sherlock Holmes story
[3]unravelling – coming apart
[4]hawk – shout
[5]defuse – release
[6]empathy – understanding and sharing the feelings of others

The following account, written in the 1800s, focuses on one specific neighbour, the 'old lady upstairs', and what it is like to live near her.

A Victorian newspaper article extract 'The old lady up stairs' compiled by George Burgess

She is a mysterious being; you never see her, and you hear of her perpetually[1]; she must be a complication of nerves and headaches, an invalid[2] of the most delicate order, and an Argus[3] whom
5 nothing escapes. She is the bar[4] to comfort, the extinguisher of fun. […] Everybody is afraid of her, and she is afraid of nobody.

Jenkins, newly married, gives a housewarming, in his first floor; Dobkins is asked because he can
10 sing a comic song, Miss Smith because she knows all the operas by heart; Twangle comes with his guitar, Traddles with his flute, and you are expected to bring a repertoire of jokes and good things. The bride is smilingly happy, the bridegroom jovial, and
15 all promises to go swimmingly. Dobkins begins his comic song, and roars of laughter follow.

Alas! Scarcely have the echoes died away, when rat-tat-tat at the door comes Biddy, with the request that 'If ye please, ye'll make no more
20 noise, for the old lady upstairs is very bad with nervousness, and can't abear it.'

Cold water is dashed upon the assemblage[5]. The hostess grows pale. Twangle's guitar and Traddles' flute are useless. The soprano of Miss Smith is
25 unheard. Your jokes are whispered, and no one smiles. Cake and wine are handed round stealthily, and you take leave at nine o'clock. […]

You make your way to the bachelor establishment of your cousin Twiggs.
30 You find him in despair, and after much pressing, he groans forth the reason.

'I can never stay out
35 after ten o'clock; the old lady upstairs has ordered the door to be locked at that hour, and takes the key to bed with her.' It is the old lady upstairs
40 who sows seeds of discontent and anger in the neighbourhood: she discovers that you use Dobkins' coal; that brother John stays out till three in the morning, and that sister Ann flirts shamefully. She is aware of the household expenses, and
45 reveals them to the neighbours. She will have the door open in winter, that her pet cat may freely exit, and will not allow it to be unclosed in summer on account of flies. She objects to company, and to mirth; she has no sympathy for childhood or
50 youth, for people who laugh, or sing, or dance […], and appears to live that others may not enjoy themselves. It is possible that she may have once been young, but the natural conclusion would be that she was born and will remain for ever the old
55 lady upstairs, and nothing else.

[1]perpetually – all the time
[2]invalid – unwell person
[3]Argus – a mythological giant with one hundred eyes
[4]bar – block
[5]assemblage – group of people

When comparing two texts, you can apply skills you already know from A01 and A02:

- interpreting ideas and perspectives
- analysing language and structure.

You can also compare other areas, such as what the writer's viewpoint is and the style he or she uses to convey this.

Read the opening paragraph by a student, who begins by establishing viewpoint and tone.

Both of these texts are about neighbours but they are written in different centuries and from different perspectives. 'How to get on with the neighbours' at first appears to be an objective article. With the exception of one personal paragraph, it takes an overview of the subject matter and includes statistical evidence. However, it is written in first person and includes many opinions as well as facts. On the other hand, the 19th-century text is a subjective narrative account of one particular evening. It is written in the second person from the point of view of someone who personally knows the neighbours of 'the old lady upstairs' and witnesses her anti-social behaviour.

Activity 1

The student answer above does not include evidence or explanations to support the good points made. Write out each of the highlighted points made. Then extend each one to make a PEE paragraph by:

• finding evidence from the relevant article to support each point.

• adding explanations to explain the effect of the writers adopting these different methods. You might consider some of the following effects to include in your explanations:

> **involving the reader**

> **demonstrating first-hand knowledge of the topic**

> **convincing the reader of the truth of the article**

> **interesting the reader in a variety of views**

> **interesting the reader in real-life stories**

> **demonstrating a fair viewpoint about a topic**

Activity 2

a Find some examples of the anti-social behaviour of neighbours in both texts.

b One way that people react to bad neighbours in the first text is to move house.

  i What other way do they react?

  ii What is the writer's attitude towards these reactions?

c One way that people react to their bad neighbour in the second text is that 'cake and wine are handed round stealthily' (lines 19 to 20).

  i What other ways do they react, and what does this suggest about them?

  ii How are these reactions different from the first text?

d How does each writer try to explain the reasoning behind the neighbours' anti-social behaviour? Which explanation do you find more convincing?

Tip ✓

Remember that as well as identifying ideas and perspectives you must interpret them to explain your understanding.

Another skill you need to show for AO3 is an ability to compare the writers' use of language. You must:

- select examples appropriately
- analyse the words, phrases, language features or sentence forms
- be precise when commenting on the effect on the reader.

Activity 3

a The first text uses several examples of colloquial (conversational) language, for example, in the opening sentence, 'If ever a statistic leapt out and hit me between the eyes…'.

   i Find some other examples of colloquial language.

   ii Which of the following descriptions of tone most accurately link to the writer's use of colloquial language? Explain the reasons for your choice.

b Read again lines 1 to 5 in the second text (page 184). The old lady is described as 'a complication of nerves and headaches' and 'an Argus whom nothing escapes'.

   i What effect do these metaphors create in the reader?

   ii Can you find any other examples of effective metaphors in this opening paragraph?

   iii How do the sentence forms add to the effect created?

Another of the skills you have to demonstrate in AO3 is to compare the writers' use of structure. Remember, you can comment on the structure of the whole text, the paragraphs or the sentences.

Activity 4

a The first text presents a logical argument to the reader.

 i Summarize the writer's view in one sentence.

 ii How does the whole text structure influence the reader to support the writer's point of view?

 iii How does this compare with the whole text structure of the second text?

b Look at the following extracts. Comment on their different sentence forms and effects.

> Personally, I have had a very mixed bag of neighbours. Some have become good friends, while others held all-night Abba parties, built dodgy extensions, chucked cigarette-ends over the garden fence and had miniature poodles who bayed like the Hound of the Baskervilles.

> Alas. Scarcely have the echoes died away, when rat-tat-tat at the door comes Biddy, with the request that 'If ye please, ye'll make no more noise, for the old lady upstairs is very bad with nervousness, and can't abear it.
>
> Cold water is dashed upon the assemblage.

Activity 5

Using all the work you have done so far on AO3, write your response to the following:

> Compare how the writers convey the subject of neighbours. Use your own words but also quote from both texts to support what you say.

Assessment Objective 4 (AO4)

Evaluate texts critically and support this with appropriate textual references.

Put simply, this means you must make an informed judgement about a text and how it is written. Your judgement must be backed up with evidence.

Where is AO4 tested in the exam?
- Paper 1, Question 4

The following extract is the opening of a short story called 'Next Term, We'll Mash You', written in 1978 by Penelope Lively. The parents of seven-year-old Charles are taking him to visit a private Sussex boarding school. They have arranged to meet with the Headmaster and his wife.

Extract from 'Next Term, We'll Mash You' by Penelope Lively

Inside the car it was quiet, the noise of the engine even and subdued, the air just the right temperature, the windows tight-fitting. The boy sat on the back seat, a box of chocolates, unopened, beside him, and a comic, folded. The trim Sussex landscape flowed past the windows: cows,

5   white-fenced fields, highly-priced period houses. The sunlight was glassy, remote[1] as a coloured photograph. The backs of the two heads in front of him swayed with the motion of the car.

His mother half-turned to speak to him. 'Nearly there now, darling.'

The father glanced downwards at his wife's wrist. 'Are we all right for time?'

10   'Just right, nearly twelve.'

'I could do with a drink. Hope they lay something on.'

'I'm sure they will. The Wilcoxes say they're awfully nice people.
15   Not really the schoolmaster-type at all, Sally says.'

The man said, 'He's an Oxford chap[2]'.

'Is he? You didn't say.'

20   'Mmn.'

'Of course, the fees are that much higher than the Seaford place.'

'Fifty quid or so. We'll have to see.'

25 The car turned right, between white gates and high, dark tight-clipped hedges. The whisper of the road under the tyres changed to the crunch of gravel. The child, staring sideways, read black lettering on a white board: *St. Edward's Preparatory School. Please Drive Slowly.* He shifted on the seat, and the leather sucked at the bare skin under his knees, stinging.

30 The mother said, 'It's a lovely place. Those must be the playing-fields. Look darling, there are some of the boys.' She clicked open her handbag, and the sun caught her mirror and flashed in the child's eyes; the comb went through her hair and he saw the grooves it left, neat as distant ploughing[3].

'Come on then, Charles, out you get.' The building was red brick, early
35 nineteenth century, spreading out long arms in which windows glittered blackly. Flowers, trapped in neat beds, were alternate red and white. They went up the steps, the man, the woman, and the child, two paces behind.

The woman, the mother, smoothing down a skirt that would be ridged from sitting, thought: I like the way they've got the maid all done up properly. The
40 little white apron and all that. She's foreign, I suppose. Au pair. Very nice. If he comes here there'll be Speech Days and that kind of thing. Sally Wilcox says it's quite dressy – she got that cream linen coat for coming down here. You can see why it costs a bomb. Great big grounds and only an hour and a half from London.

45 They went into a room looking out onto a terrace. Beyond, dappled lawns, gently shifting trees, black and white cows grazing behind iron railings. Books, leather chairs, a table with magazines – *Country Life, The Field, The Economist.* 'Please, if you would wait here. The Headmaster won't be long.'

Alone, they sat, inspected. 'I like the atmosphere, don't you, John?'

50 'Very pleasant, yes.' Four hundred a term, near enough. You can tell it's a cut above the Seaford place, though, or the one at St Albans. Bob Wilcox says quite a few City people send their boys here. One or two of the merchant bankers[4], those kind of people. It's the sort of contact that would do no harm at all. You meet someone, get talking at a cricket match or what have you...
55 Not at all a bad thing.

'All right, Charles? You didn't get sick in the car, did you?'

The child had black hair, slicked down smooth to his head. His ears, too large, jutted out, transparent[5] in the light from the window, laced with tiny, delicate veins. His clothes had the shine and crease of newness. He looked at the
60 books, the dark brown pictures, his parents. Said nothing.

[1]remote – distant
[2]an Oxford chap – someone who went to Oxford University
[3]ploughing – rows in fields
[4]merchant bankers – bankers who trade with goods and investments, often wealthy
[5]transparent – see through

Tip ✓

One way of evaluating a text is to organize your comments around characters and events. You can use interpretation of events and analysis of language and structure to support them.

We learn a lot about the characters in this extract through:

- the things they say and do
- the way they interact with one other
- the language used to describe the characters.

Before you answer the questions below, decide on your impression of the boy Charles and how the writer conveys him.

Activity 1

a Read the first paragraph again.

  i Why is it important that the box of chocolates is 'unopened' and the comic 'folded'?

  ii What are your initial impressions of Charles from these details and the rest of this opening paragraph?

b As the car drives into the grounds of the school we are told: 'He shifted on the seat, and the leather sucked at the bare skin under his knees, stinging' (lines 28 to 29). What does the writer's choice of language suggest about Charles at this point?

c When Charles and his parents enter the school building we learn: 'They went up the steps, the man, the woman, and the child, two paces behind' (lines 36 to 37). What does this suggest about the relationships between the family members?

d Charles says nothing in this extract, although it is easy to miss this fact when reading the story. Why are the final two words 'Said nothing' placed at the end? How does the physical description of Charles in the final paragraph add to our understanding of him?

On the surface, the character of the mother appears to be caring and attentive, but there are hints throughout the text that she may be more concerned with herself than her son. Complete Activity 2 on page 191 to explore this.

Activity 2

a Look at the dialogue spoken by the mother.

   i How does it influence your impression of her?

   ii What does it suggest about her relationship with her husband and her son?

b Read again lines 30 to 34.

   i What do her actions suggest about her character?

   ii Where else in the extract is the same impression created?

c When the mother tends to her hair, the grooves from the comb are described as 'neat as distant ploughing'. What does this simile suggest about the mother and the situation?

d Read again lines 38 to 44.

   i Thinking about how the text is organized, why is it significant to learn of her thoughts at this point in the text?

   ii How much do you think she cares what is best for Charles?

On the surface, the character of the father is similar to the mother. However, the writer hints that the welfare of his son is not his main concern.

Activity 3

a Look at the dialogue spoken by the father.

   i How does it influence your impression of him?

   ii What does it suggest about his relationship with his wife and his son?

b Read again lines 50 to 55.

   i Thinking about how the text is built, why is it significant to learn of his thoughts at this point in the text?

   ii How concerned do you think he is about Charles' best interests?

The writer uses the setting to support our understanding of characters and events. She creates contrast by combining ideas of attractiveness and imprisonment.

Idyllic setting	Threatening prison-like setting
● 'white-fenced' fields ● 'highly-priced period houses'	● 'tight fitting' car windows ● 'The building was red brick, early nineteenth century, spreading out long arms' ● 'in which windows glittered blackly'

Activity 4

a Find some other examples in the text that make the setting appear to be perfect. How does this affect our first impression of the place?

b Find some other examples of words, phrases or language features that suggest a feeling of being trapped. How might this change our first impression of the place?

c Find some other examples of images where the initial positive impression is then twisted into something negative.

Activity 5

Using all the work you have done on AO4, write your response to the following question:

The title of this story is 'Next Term, We'll Mash You'. This is a comment made to Charles by one of the pupils during his visit, threatening to bully him if he joins the school.

To what extent does the opening extract prepare you, the reader, for this undercurrent of unpleasantness?

Assessment Objectives 5 and 6 (AO5, AO6)

AO5 Communicate clearly, effectively and imaginatively, selecting and adapting tone, style and register for different forms, purposes and audiences.
Organize information and ideas, using structural and grammatical features to support coherence and cohesion of texts.

AO6 Use a range of vocabulary and sentence structure for clarity, purpose and effect, with accurate spelling and punctuation.

Put simply, these objectives focus on your writing. You should write accurate, structured, appropriate texts to interest your reader.

Where are AO5 and AO6 tested in the exam?
• Paper 1, Question 5, where you have to narrate or describe
• Paper 2, Question 5, where you have to explain your point of view on a given statement

Tip ✔

Remember to think about:
• text type
• audience
• purpose.

Make sure that you:
• vary your sentence structures
• use correct spelling and punctuation
• write in Standard English.

There are three stages to any response:
• planning
• writing
• proofreading.

Paper 1
Narrative writing

Use your imagination. Plan your:

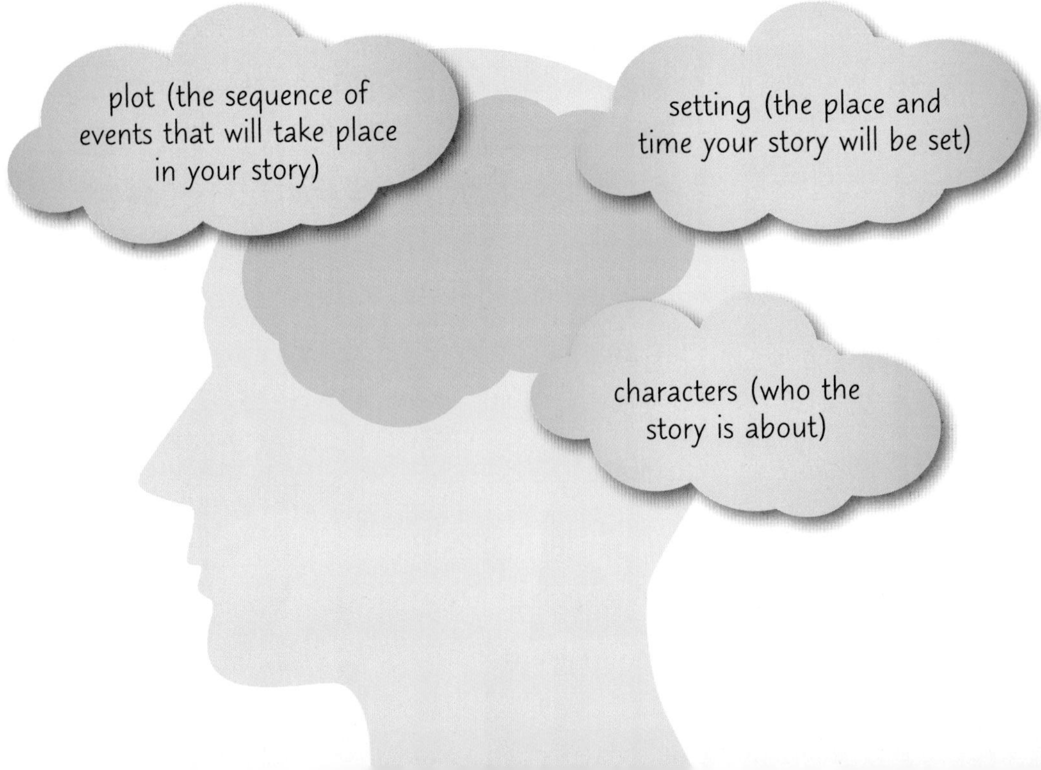

plot (the sequence of events that will take place in your story)

setting (the place and time your story will be set)

characters (who the story is about)

Activity 1

Look at the image below and start to use your imagination. Make notes on the plot, setting and characters for your story.

Decide on:

- viewpoint (who is narrating the story)
- structure (how the story will begin, what conflict will be encountered by your characters and how it will be resolved)
- mood or atmosphere.

Activity 2

Make notes on the viewpoint, structure and mood for your story.

You must think carefully about how you craft your language.

You might engage your reader through:

- vocabulary choices (choose a bank of interesting words related to your topic)
- descriptive detail (to convey setting or character)
- dialogue (but not too much)
- action (detailing events to move the story on).

Activity 3

a Make a note of any words, phrases or language features that you could include in your story to engage your reader.

b Using all the work you have done so far on AO5, write a full narrative suggested by the picture above.

For AO6 you need to:

- use a range of appropriate sentence forms
- punctuate your narrative correctly
- write in Standard English.

Read through your narrative written in Activity 3b, to check it is clear and accurate. Make any changes that would improve your demonstration of AO6 skills.

Descriptive writing

A description is a picture made up of words. A successful description helps your reader to: share your vision; see the place in your mind's eye. The steps below can be followed when writing descriptively.

1. Jot down ideas on the five senses: what can you hear, see, smell, taste, touch?

2. Organize your ideas and decide how to structure them:

- in the order of importance
- the time order in which events occur
- by the different places they are set.

3. Craft your description. Engage your reader through:

- Choice of language: specific adjectives and adverbs and powerful verbs that bring the description to life
- Imagery: similes and metaphors
- Tone: how can the sound and images of the words you choose support this?

> ### Activity 4
>
> **a** Look at the image below. Make notes on how you could apply the above bullet points to a description of your own.
>
> **b** Using your notes, write a description suggested by this picture.
>
> **c** Read through your description to check what you have written is clear and accurate. Make any changes that would improve your AO6 skills.

Key terms

Fact: something that can be proved to be true

Anecdote: a short relevant story about an apparently real incident or person

Emotive language: words and phrases that are deliberately used to provoke an emotional reaction

Rhetorical question: a question asked for dramatic effect and not intended to get an answer

Figurative language: imaginative language that is used to convey an idea. It can use a comparison or a sound, for interest, or to illustrate an idea rather than stating it explicitly. Examples include simile, metaphor, personification and alliteration

Paper 2

In Paper 2, explain your point of view on a given statement. You will need to:

- decide what your opinion is on the given statement
- think about the reasons why you hold this point of view.

Tip ✓

It is useful to consider any alternative viewpoints so that you can mention them, dismiss them in your response and strengthen your argument.

Activity 5

Read the following statement and decide if you agree with it, disagree with it or agree with it in some ways but not others.

A research scientist recently said: 'We have no idea of the long term impact of mobile phones, and therefore they should not be used by anyone under the age of 18.'

Plan your answer. You will need to:

- list reasons for and against this statement
- think of as many aspects as you can, for example, enjoyment, health, communication, privacy, etc.
- select two or three main reasons that support your point of view that you can discuss and develop in detail.

Tip ✓

Discuss each of your reasons in a separate paragraph.

For AO5 you must organize your essay.

Activity 6

Plan your response to this task:

Write a letter of reply to the research scientist in which you explain your point of view on the statement given above.

You must convince your reader to agree with you. Remember to include:

- evidence in the form of other people's opinions, **facts** or **anecdotes**
- effective vocabulary choices and language features, such as language for **emotive** effect, **rhetorical questions**, **figurative language**, or repetition.

Tip ✓

Open your piece with a strong introduction. You might choose:

- a minor sentence
- a question
- a direct address to the audience
- an anecdote.

Activity 7

a Make a note of any evidence you could offer in support of your point of view.

b Note any *effective vocabulary choices* to include in your letter to convince your reader.

c Note any *language features* to include in your letter to convince your reader.

d Using all the work you have done so far on AO5, write a letter in response to the given statement.

e Read through your letter to check that what you have written is clear and accurate. Make any changes that would show a higher level of skill for AO6.

Full sample papers

Paper 1: Explorations in creative reading and writing

Source A

This extract is the opening of a short story by John Wyndham. Although written in 1952, it is set in the future. In this section, a shuttle bus is taking the next group of volunteers to a space ship, ready to depart for Mars.

Survival

As the spaceport bus trundled unhurriedly over the mile or more of open field that separated the terminal building from the embarkation hoist[1], Mrs Feltham stared intently forward across the
5   receding[2] row of shoulders in front of her.

The ship stood up on the plain like an isolated silver spire. Near its bow she could see the intense blue light which proclaimed it all but ready to take off. Among and around the great tail fins,
10   dwarf vehicles and little dots of men moved in a fuss of final preparations. Mrs Feltham glared at the scene, at this moment loathing[3] it and all the inventions of men with a hard, hopeless hatred.

Presently she withdrew her gaze from the distance
15   and focused it on the back of her son-in-law's head, a yard in front of her. She hated him, too.

She turned, darting a swift glance at the face of her daughter in the seat beside her. Alice looked pale; her lips were firmly set, her eyes fixed straight
20   ahead.

Mrs Feltham hesitated. Her glance returned to the spaceship. She decided on one last effort. Under cover of the bus noise, she said: 'Alice, darling, it's not too late, even now, you know.'

25   The girl did not look at her. There was no sign that she had heard, save that her lips compressed[4] a little more firmly. Then they parted.

'Mother, please!' she said.

But Mrs Feltham, once started, had to go on.

'It's for your own sake, darling. All you have to do is 30 say you've changed your mind.'

The girl held a protesting silence.

'Nobody would blame you,' Mrs Feltham persisted. 'They'd not think a bit worse of you. After all, everybody knows that Mars is no place for –' 35

'Mother, please stop it,' interrupted the girl.

The sharpness of her tone took Mrs Feltham aback for a moment. She hesitated. But time was growing too short to allow herself the luxury of offended dignity. She went on: 'You're not used to the sort 40 of life you'll have to live there, darling. Absolutely primitive. No kind of life for any woman. After all, dear, it is only a five year appointment for David. I'm sure if he really loves you he'd rather know that you are safe here and waiting –' 45

The girl said, harshly: 'We've been over all this before, Mother. I tell you it's no good. I'm not a child. I've thought it out, and I've made up my mind.'

Mrs Feltham sat silent for some moments. The bus swayed on across the field, and the rocketship 50 seemed to tower further into the sky.

'If you had a child of your own –' she said, half to herself. 'Well, I expect some day you will. Then you will begin to understand…'

[1]embarkation hoist – take off platform for the space ship
[2]receding – going back from a certain point
[3]loathing – hating
[4]compressed – squeezed together

Section A: Reading

1 Read again the first part of the source, lines 1 to 5.

List **four** things from this part of the text about Mrs Feltham's journey.

[4 marks]

2 Look in detail at this extract from lines 6 to 16 of the source:

> The ship stood up on the plain like an isolated silver spire. Near its bow she could see the intense blue light which proclaimed it all but ready to take off. Among and around the great tail fins, dwarf vehicles and little dots of men moved in a fuss of final preparations. Mrs Feltham glared at the scene, at this moment loathing it and all the inventions of men with a hard, hopeless hatred.
>
> Presently she withdrew her gaze from the distance and focused it on the back of her son-in-law's head, a yard in front of her. She hated him, too.

How does the writer use language here to describe the space ship and Mrs Feltham's response to it?

You could include the writer's choice of:

- words and phrases

- language features and techniques

- sentence forms.

[8 marks]

3 You now need to think about the whole of the source.

This text is from the opening of a short story.

How has the writer structured the text to interest you as a reader?

You could write about:

- what the writer focuses your attention on at the beginning

- how and why the writer changes this focus as the extract develops

- any other structural features that interest you.

[8 marks]

4 Focus this part of your answer on the rest of the source, from line 17 to the end.

A novelist once said: 'Mothers and daughters with strong personalities might see the world from very different points of view.'

To what extent do you agree?

In your response, you should:

- write about what impressions Mrs Feltham and Alice make on the reader

- evaluate how the writer has created these impressions

- support your opinions with quotations from the text.

[20 marks]

5 You are going to enter a creative writing competition.

Either:

Write a description suggested by this picture:

Or

Write a story about tension between a mother and daughter.

(24 marks for content and organization,

16 marks for technical accuracy)

[40 marks]

Paper 2: Writers' viewpoints and perspectives

Source A

The following newspaper article was written by Tanith Carey, a parenting expert, in response to the Channel 4 programme, *Child Genius.*

Cruellest reality TV show ever

At the tender age of eight, Tudor Mendel-Idowu has been picked to play soccer for no fewer than three Premier League junior teams: QPR, Tottenham and Chelsea. This achievement alone would be enough to make most fathers' hearts burst with pride. But, unfortunately for Tudor, he appears to have a very long way to go before he meets the sky-high expectations of his demanding dad, Tolu.

5   So far, the most heart-rending scenes on Channel 4's reality series Child Genius – in which 20 gifted children are subjected to a terrifying barrage[1] of tests – have been the sight of this small boy hiding his face in his hands as he weeps. The reason? He has not scored as well as his father tells him he should have done. [...] Yet rather than commiserate[2] with his son after a disappointing performance, it is Tolu, who declares that he finds the contest 'emotionally draining'. He then tells
10   Tudor: 'Maybe you're not as good as we thought.' [...]

Even for a nation well used to the mercenary[3] exploitation of spy-on-the-wall television, this has raised concern. As one worried viewer pointed out, the series would more aptly be named 'Lunatic Parents'. For it is really all about the Eagle Dads and Tiger Mums, who want to show off how much work they have invested in their youngsters.

15   The show first aired in its current format last year, and – as the author of a book looking at the damage caused by competitive parenting – I had thought we would not see a return of this toxic[4] mix of reality TV and hot-housing[5]. I had expected the sight of children as young as eight crying to prick the conscience of the commissioning editors[6].

A vain hope, of course. [...]

20   Child Genius has tapped into an increasingly dangerous trend in parenting; the misguided[7] belief that your offspring is a blank slate and if you hot-house them enough, you can be solely responsible for their success. Parenting is turning into a form of product development. Increasingly, we are falling for the notion that if we cram enough facts into their little brains we can make sure they come out on top. The end result is a rise in depression and anxiety among a generation who
25   believe they are losers if they fail, or could always do better if they win.

Like all offspring of pushy parents, who feel their family's affection is conditional[8] on their success, children like Tudor are not just weeping because they didn't score well. When he tries to cover his tears with his hands, saying 'What I achieved was absolutely terrible', he is facing a much darker fear: That he will lose his father's love if he does not come up to scratch. [...]

30   Of course, the goal of reality TV is to entertain — but should dramatic story-lines really come ahead of a child's emotional well-being?

Perhaps it's a measure of their state of mind that some parents, such as psychologists Shoshana and Sacha, who featured in the first two episodes, saw nothing harmful in describing their approach to bringing up their daughter Aliyah, nine, as though she is 'a well-bred race-horse'.
35   Shoshana openly pities parents left to bring up children without her skill set. She was blissfully oblivious to the fact that the rest of us were watching, slack-jawed in disbelief at how hard she pushes her child. Far from rushing to adopt such techniques, parents have reacted in horror. The internet has been buzzing with viewers saying they found the series 'upsetting to watch', 'heartbreaking' and expressing concern that it 'verges on abuse'. [...]

40   No doubt the reality is that Tolu is also a loving father, who sincerely believes he is doing the best for his son, and the producers have edited the programme to make him look like the ultimate caricature of an overbearing father.

But for me, one question remains: How much longer are we going to allow Channel 4 to

45 encourage extreme parents to push their helpless children to breaking point in the name of entertainment?

[1]barrage – battering
[2]commiserate – sympathize
[3]mercenary – money-grabbing
[4]toxic – poisonous
[5]hot-housing – intensely educating a gifted child
[6]commissioning editors – people in charge of the programme

[7]misguided – wrong
[8]conditional – dependent

Source B

The following newspaper article was written in the 19th century. It also offers views on how to raise children.

Children

It is a mistake to think that children love the parents less who maintain a proper authority over them. On the contrary, they respect them more. It is a cruel and unnatural selfishness that indulges children in a foolish and hurtful way. Parents are guides and counsellors to their children. As a guide in a foreign
5 land, they undertake to pilot them safely through the shoals and quicksands[1] of inexperience. If the guide allows his followers all the freedom they please; if, because they dislike the constraint of the narrow path of safety, he allows them to stray into holes and precipices[2] that destroy them, to quench their thirst in brooks that poison them, to loiter[3] in woods full or wild beasts of deadly herbs,
10 can he be called a sure guide?

And is it not the same with our children? They are as yet only in the preface, or as it were, in the first chapter of the book of life. We have nearly finished it, or are far advanced. We must open the pages for these younger minds.

If children see that their parents act from principle – that they do not find
15 fault without reason – that they do not punish because personal offence is taken, but because the thing in itself is wrong – if they see that while they are resolutely but affectionately refused what is not good for them, there is a willingness to oblige them in all innocent matters – they will soon appreciate such conduct. If no attention is paid to the rational wishes – if no allowance is
20 made for youthful spirits – if they are dealt with in a hard and unsympathising manner – the proud spirit will rebel, and the meek spirit be broken. […]

A pert[4] or improper way of speaking ought never to be allowed. Clever children are very apt to be pert, and if too much admired for it, and laughed at, become eccentric and disagreeable. It is often very difficult to check our
25 own amusement, but their future welfare should be regarded more than our present entertainment. It should never be forgotten that they are tender plants committed to our fostering[5] care, that every thoughtless word or careless neglect may destroy a germ of immortality[6].

[1]shoals and quicksands – bewildering choices and dangers (metaphors)
[2]precipices – steep, dangerous places
[3]loiter – linger
[4]pert – cheeky
[5]fostering – nurturing and protective
[6]immortality – living for ever

Section A: Reading

1 Read again **source A**, *Cruellest reality TV show ever*, from lines 1 to 10.

Choose **four** statements below which are TRUE.   **[4 marks]**

- Shade the boxes of the ones that you think are true.

- Choose a maximum of four statements.

A. Tudor has been picked to play soccer for three Premier League junior teams.

B. Tolu's heart is bursting with pride at his son's achievements.

C. Child Genius is a TV programme on Channel 3.

D. Tudor hides his face in his hands as he weeps.

E. Tudor does not score as well as his father thinks he should.

F. Tolu sympathizes with Tudor over his disappointing performance.

G. Tudor finds the contest emotionally draining.

H. Tudor may not be as good as his father thought.

2 You need to refer to the whole of **source A** and **source B**, lines 22 to 28 for this question.

Use details from **both** sources. Write a summary of the different ways to raise a child who is clever.   **[8 marks]**

3 You now need to refer only to **source B**, *Children*, lines 1 to 13.

How does the writer use language to describe the role of parents?   **[12 marks]**

4 For this question, you need to refer to the whole of **source A** and the whole of **source B**.

Compare the two writers' views on raising children.

In your answer, you should:

- compare the different viewpoints of the writers

- compare the methods the writers use to convey these viewpoints

- support your ideas with quotations from both texts.   **[16 marks]**

Section B: Writing

5 'Children need strict discipline from their parents when they are young or they will grow into teenagers who are out of control.'

Write a magazine article in which you explain your point of view on this statement.

(24 marks for content and organization,

16 marks for technical accuracy)

[40 marks]

Glossary

Abstract noun: a word that identifies things that cannot be physically touched or seen, such as an idea, a state or a feeling

Adjective: a word that describes something named by a noun or pronoun

Adverb: a word used to describe verbs, adjectives or other adverbs

Audience: the person or people you are writing for, for example, readers of a magazine, listeners of a radio programme, your head teacher

Clause: a group of words that include a verb. Sentences can be made up of one or more clauses

Common noun: a common noun identifies a person, place or thing, but does not need a capital letter (unlike a proper noun, which gives the name of a specific person, place or organization)

Complex sentence: a complex sentence is made up of a main clause with one or more subordinate clauses dependent on it. A subordinate clause can start with words such as *although, because, so*

Compound sentence: a compound sentence is made up of two of more simple sentences joined together using a connective such as *and* or *but*

Connective: a word that joins phrases or sentences, such as *moreover, as a result, furthermore, in addition, not only… but also, because, therefore, consequently*

Connotation: an idea or feeling suggested, in addition to the main meaning. For example, the connotations of the word 'beach' might be sunshine or gritty sand, depending on your experience of the beach

Dialogue: a conversation between two or more people. There are many reasons why writers use dialogue in their stories, including:
- to help the reader to understand more about the characters
- to show how different characters interact
- to move the plot forward
- to break up the action of the story

Emotive language: words and phrases that are deliberately used to provoke an emotional reaction

Explicit: clearly stated; you just need to find it

Figurative language: imaginative language that is used to convey an idea. It can use a comparison or a sound, for interest, or to illustrate an idea rather than stating it explicitly. Examples include simile, metaphor, personification and alliteration

First-person pronouns: *I* and *we* are first-person pronouns

First-person narrative: story or account told from the point of view of a character or one of the people involved, typically using the pronouns *I* and *we*

Implicit: suggested; you have to interpret the text to work it out for yourself

Interpret: explain the meaning of something in your own words, showing your understanding

Metaphor: a comparison showing the similarity between two quite different things, stating that one actually is the other

Mood: the feeling or atmosphere created by a piece of writing

Nouns: nouns identify a person, place or thing

Objective: a perspective not influenced by personal feelings of opinions

Purpose: the reason why you are writing, for example, to argue, to persuade, to offer a point of view

Register: the kind of words (for example, formal, informal, literary) and the manner of speaking or writing; these vary according to the situation and the relationship of the people involved

Reporting clause: the part of the sentence that tells us who spoke and how they said it. For example, *he shouted, she muttered*
Rhetorical question: a question asked for dramatic effect and not intended to get an answer

Rhetorical question: a question asked for dramatic effect and not intended to get an answer

Second-person narrative: story or account told from the point of view of the reader, typically using the pronoun *you*

Setting: the place or surroundings where an event takes place or something is positioned

Simile: a comparison showing the similarity between two different things, stating that one is like the other

Structure: organize the text, including an introduction, headings, subheadings, lists, and grouping ideas into paragraphs

Subjective: a perspective influenced by personal feelings or opinions

Summarize: to give the main points of something briefly.

Suspense and tension: the feeling of waiting, as though something is about to happen

Synonyms: words with similar meanings

Synthesize: to combine information and ideas from different texts

Text type: the type of writing, for example, an article, a letter, a leaflet

Tone: a way of writing which conveys the writer's attitude towards either the reader or the subject matter

Third-person narrative: story or account told from the point of view of an 'outsider', a narrator who is not a directly involved, typically using the pronouns *he, she, it* and *they*

Verbs: words that mark actions, events, processes and states. They usually have a tense, either present, past or future

OXFORD
UNIVERSITY PRESS

Great Clarendon Street, Oxford, OX2 6DP,
United Kingdom

Oxford University Press is a department of the University of Oxford.

It furthers the University's objective of excellence in research, scholarship, and education by publishing worldwide. Oxford is a registered trade mark of Oxford University Press in the UK and in certain other countries

First published in 2015

British Library Cataloguing in Publication Data

Data available

ISBN 978-019-835904-3

10 9 8 7 6 5 4 3 2

Printed in China by Sheck Wah Tong Printing Press Ltd

Acknowledgements

The authors and publisher are grateful for permission to reprint extracts from the following copyright material:

Peter Ackroyd: *Hawksmoor* (Hamish Hamilton, 1985), copyright © Peter Ackroyd 1985, reprinted by permission of Penguin Books Ltd.

Monica Ali: *Brick Lane* (Doubleday, 2003), copyright © Monica Ali 2003, reprinted by permission of The Random House Group Ltd

Floella Benjamin: *Coming to England: An Autobiography* (Walker Books, 2009), copyright © Floella Benjamin 1995, 2009, reprinted by permission of Benjamin-Taylor Associates.

Ray Bradbury: 'The Pedestrian' copyright © 1951 by the Fortnightly Publishing Company, © renewed 1979 by Ray Bradbury, first published in *The Reporter*, Aug 1951, from *The Golden Apples of the Sun* (Bantam Books, 1954), reprinted by permission of Abner Stein.

Xan Brooks: review of *The Woman in Black*, *The Guardian*, 9 Feb 2012,copyright © Guardian News & Media Ltd 2012, reprinted by permission of Guardian News & Media Ltd.

Tanith Carey: 'Cruellest reality TV show ever', *Daily Mail*, 3 Aug 2014, copyright © Daily Mail 2014, reprinted by permission of Solo Syndication/Daily Mail.

Rachel Carlyle: 'A Bug's life: Bed bugs are back and living under a mattress near you!', *The Express*, 5 Feb 2013, reprinted by permission of Express Newspapers.

Angela Carter: 'The Werewolf' from Burning Your Boats: the collected short stories Chatto & Windus, 1995), copyright © Angela Carter 1979, reprinted by permission of reprinted by permission of the author c/o Rogers, Coleridge & White Ltd, 20 Powis Mews, London W11 1\JN.

Max Davidson: 'How to get on with your neighbours', *Daily Telegraph*, 5 Aug 2011, copyright © Telegraph Media Group Ltd 2011, reprinted by permission of TMG.

Alex Hannaford: '127 Hours: Aron Ralston's story of survival', *The Telegraph*, 6 Jan 2011, copyright © Telegraph Media Group Ltd 2011, reprinted by permission of TMG.

Simon Hattestone: 'Tales of the City' 11 Aug 2003, copyright © Guardian News & Media Ltd 2003, reprinted by permission of Guardian News & Media Ltd.

Eugene Henderson: 'I've got it nice says killer as he brags of easy life in jail', *The Express*, 24 June 2012, reprinted by permission of Express Newspapers.

Patricia Highsmith: 'The snail watcher' from *Eleven* (Bloomsbury, 2007), copyright © Patricia Highsmith 1970, reprinted by permission of the Little Brown Book Group Ltd by arrangement with Diogenes Verlag AG

Amelia Hill: 'Why we love sounds of the city jungle', *The Observer*, 23 Sept 2007, copyright © Guardian News & Media Ltd 2007, reprinted by permission of Guardian News & Media Ltd.

Susan Hill: *The Man in the Picture* (Profile Books, 2012), copyright © Susan Hill 2007, reprinted by permission of the publishers.

Dr Martin Luther King Jr: 'I Have a Dream', spoken at a Civil Rights rally in Washington DC, 1963, copyright © 1963 Dr Martin Luther King Jr, © renewed 1991 by Coretta Scott King, reprinted by arrangement with the Heirs to the Estate of Martin Luther King Jr., c/o Writers House as agent for the proprietor, New York, NY, USA.

Laurie Lee: *Cider with Rosie* (Vintage, 2011), copyright © Laurie Lee 1959, reprinted by permission of the Curtis Brown Group Ltd, London on behalf of the Beneficiaries of The Estate of Laurie Lee.

Penelope Lively: 'Next Term, We'll Mash You' from *Pack of Cards: Stories 1978-1986* (Penguin, 1987), copyright © Penelope Lively 1987, reprinted by permission of David Higham Associates.

David Mitchell: introduction to *The Reason I Jump: One Boy's Voice from the Silence of Autism* by Naoki Higashida, translated by David Mitchell and Keiki Yoshida (Sceptre, 2013), introduction copyright © David Mitchell 2013, reprinted by permission of Hodder & Stoughton Ltd.

George Orwell: *Nineteen Eighty-Four* (Viking, 2008), copyright © George Orwell 1949, reprinted by permission A M Heath & Co Ltd, Authors' Agents on behalf of Bill Hamilton as the Literary Executor of the Estate of the Late Sonia Brownell Orwell.

Tony Parsons: 'Making my skin crawl: Tattoos scream for attention', *The Mirror*, 23 June 2012, copyright © Tony Parson 2012, reprinted by permission of Curtis Brown Group Ltd , London, on be of Tony Parsons,

Terry Pratchett: 'Those of us with Dementia need a little help from our friends', *The Guardian*, 13 M 2014, reprinted by permission of Colin Smythe on behalf of the author.

Ross Raisin: *God's Own Country* (Viking, 2008), copyright © Ross Raisin 2008, reprinted by permissic Penguin Books Ltd.

Jon Ronson: *The Pyschopath Test: a journey through the madness industry* (Picador, 2011), copyright © Jon Ronson 2011, reprinted by permission of the publishers, Pan Macmillan UK.

Paullina Simons: *Eleven Hours* (Flamingo, 1998), copyright © Paullina Simons 1998, reprinted by permission of HarperCollins Publishers Ltd.

John Wyndham: 'Survival' from *The Seeds of Time* (Penguin, 1959), reprinted by permission of Davic Higham Associates.

Benjamin Zephaniah: 'Me? I thought, OBE me? Up Yours, I thought', *The Guardian*, 27 Nov 2003, copyright © Benjamin Zephaniah 2003, reprinted by permission of United Agents (www.unitedage co.uk), on behalf of Benjamin Zephaniah.

and to the following for their permission to reprint extracts from copyright material:

The Queen's Printer for Scotland for extract from 'Just because they're sold as legal, doesn't m they're safe' from *Know the Score*, the national drugs helpline for Scotland, a Scottish Government website, © Crown Copyright, reprinted under the Open Government Licence.

ITN (Independent Televison News) for Lawrence McGinty interview 'Stephen Hawking: I'm a scientist not a celebrity', ITV News, 16 Sept 2013.

Solo Syndication/MailOnline for 'Autumnwatch presenter Chris Packam slams I'm a Celebrity f "killing animals and cruelty to bugs and insects"', MailOnline, 3 Dec 2009, copyright © Daily Mail 2009.

Stonewall for 'FA and Premier League slammed by fans for failure to tackle anti-gays abuse', from www.stonewall.org.uk/media.

Telegraph Media Group Ltd for 'Rare Amnesia leaves mother with 17 year memory gap', *The Telegraph*, 29 July 2011, copyright © Telegraph Media Group Ltd 2011.

The authors and publisher would like to thank the following for permission to use their photograp

Cover: © imageBROKER/Alamy; **p10:** (t) Tomatito/Shutterstock, (b) © Olga Khoroshunova/Alamy; **p11:** (tr) Akil Rolle-Rowan/Shutterstock, (ml) Mirek Kijewski/Shutterstock, (mr) MitchR/Shutterstoc (bl) konmesa/Shutterstock, (br) Nekrasov Andrey/Shutterstock; **p12:** © Jack Sullivan/Alamy; **p13:** Vorobyeva/Shutterstock; **p14:** © Beth Dixson/Alamy; **p15:** ITV/REX; **p16:** Mr. SUTTIPON YAKHAM/ Shutterstock; **p17:** jaboo2foto/Shutterstock; **p18:** © Life on white/Alamy; **p19:** © David Page/ Alamy; **p20:** © Bon Appetit/Alamy; **p21:** GlobalP/iStockphoto; **p22-23:** © Chris Howes/Wild Places Photography/Alamy; **p24:** (background) MJTH/Shutterstock, (foreground) jps/Shutterstock; **p26-27:** Ricardo Reitmeyer/Shutterstock; **p28:** ChinaFotoPress/Getty Images; **p31:** Soyka/Shutterstock; **p33** Aleksey Stemmer/Shutterstock; **p35:** sarayuth3390/Shutterstock; **p36:** © Don Bartell/Stockimo/Ala **p38:** Tim Flach/Getty Images; **p41:** © Richard Garvey-Williams/Alamy; **p43:** © Christina Richards/ Corbis; **p44:** (t) Mary Evans/Epic/Tallandier, (b) © The British Library Board (EVAN. 2682); **p45:** (t) M Evans/The National Archives, London. England., (b) © Hulton-Deutsch Collection/CORBIS; **p47:** © Bettmann/CORBIS; **p49:** Tal/Epic/Mary Evans; **p50:** © Jeff Morgan 16/Alamy; **p51:** © Matt Limb OBE Alamy; **p52-53:** Zeljkica/Shutterstock; **p53:** © Flip Schulke/CORBIS; **p54-55:** © Catherine Ivill/AMA Matthew Ashton/AMA Sports Photo/AMA/Corbis; **p56:** (t) © Bill Cheyrou/Alamy, (bl) India Picture/ Shutterstock, (br) © PYMCA/Alamy; **p58-59:** Tatiana Kasyanova/Shutterstock; **p59:** EV040/Shutterst **p60:** © EDDIE KEOGH/Reuters/Corbis; **p61:** © CBW/Alamy; **p63:** © AF archive/Alamy; **p65:** © AF archive/Alamy; **p66:** © Dan De Kleined/Alamy; **p68:** © ZUMA Press, Inc./Alamy; **p71:** CristinaMurac Shutterstock; **p72:** With kind permission from Nami Horiike; **p75:** With kind permission from Hodder & Stoughton; **p76:** (tl) KeystoneUSA-ZUMA/REX, (r) Bill Pugliano/Getty Images, (bl) John Co Press Associates Ltd.; **p77:** (t) © eStock Photo/Alamy, (m) © veryan dale/Alamy, (b) threerocksimage Shutterstock; **p78:** © Armando Gallo/Corbis; **p79:** © Moviestore collection Ltd/Alamy; **p80:** © Phot 12/Alamy; **p82:** © Photographer: Yva Momatiuk and J/Corbis; **p83:** © Photo Researchers/Mary Evan Picture Library; **p84-85:** © liszt collection/Alamy; **p86:** Gunnar Pippel/Shutterstock; **p89:** Arthur S. Aubry/Getty Images; **p90-91:** xc/Shutterstock; **p93:** © ToreHeggelund/RooM the Agency/Corbis; **p9** Ljupco Smokovski/Shutterstock; **p96-99:** Martina Vaculikova/Shutterstock; **p96:** (t) © Photos 12/Ala (b) Tom Dymond/Comic Relief/REX; **p98:** © Eleanor Bentall/Corbis; **p100:** yakub88/Shutterstock; **p** © Sport In Pictures/Alamy; **p105:** © CORBIS; **p109:** "My Wife and My Mother-in-Law" by William Ely Hill, 1915; **p110:** (tl) © Photos 12/Alamy, (tr) © Photos 12/Alamy, (bl) © Pictorial Press Ltd/Alamy (br) Hulton Archive/Getty Images; **p111:** © Pictorial Press Ltd/Alamy; **p112:** (l) Elnur/Shutterstock, (ml) hxdbzxy/Shutterstock, (mr) Kay Welsh/Shutterstock, (r) Stephanie Connell/Shutterstock; **p113:** vesilvio/Shutterstock; p114: THE MAN IN THE PICTURE by Susan Hill is published by Profile Books; **p116-117**: agsandrew/Shutterstock; **p118:** (background) Petr84/Shutterstock, (foreground) Twin Design/Shutterstock; **p119:** David Burrows/Shutterstock; **p120:** © Cristian Gusa/Alamy; p**122-123:** Mary Evans/Library of Congress; p124: With kind permission from West Yorkshire Police; **p129:** © Feng Yu/Alamy; **p131:** CATERS News Agency; **p133:** Jeff Moore/Jeff Moore/Empics Entertainment; **p137:** (l) © Stan Kujawa/Alamy, (r) © Stan Kujawa/Alamy; **p139:** Mary Evans Picture Library; **p141:** Antony Nagelmann/Getty Images; **p142:** QQ7/Shutterstock; **p143:** Shahid Khan/Shutterstock; **p14** Eddy Galeotti/Shutterstock; **p145:** NigelSpiers/Shutterstock; **p146:** © A ROOM WITH VIEWS/Alamy **p147:** Andrei Zveaghintev/Shutterstock; **p148:** (l) Artwork © Mark Atkins/panoptica.net. Used by arrangement with The Random House Group Limited., (r) Jeremy Sutton-Hibbert/Getty Images; **p151:** © Les Stone/Sygma/Corbis; **p152-153:** Daniel J. Rao/Smhutterstock; **p155:** © Adrian Sherrat Alamy; **p157:** David Good/Shutterstock; **p159:** © Martin Almqvist/Alamy; **p160:** Photographee.eu/ Shutterstock; **p161:** pio3/Shutterstock; **p163:** Mary Evans Picture Library/HENRY GRANT; **p164:** Th Len/Shutterstock; **p164-165:** © The Protected Art Archive/Alamy; **p166:** © nobleIMAGES/Alamy; **p1** © Matthew Mawson/Alamy; **p170:** Andrew Bret Wallis/Getty Images; **p173:** British Library/Robana/ REX; **p174:** Chones/Shutterstock; **p175:** Oktay Ortakcioglu/Getty Images; **p176:** © WENN Ltd/Alam **p177:** © GL Archive/Alamy; **p178:** Mikhail Klyoshev/Shutterstock; **p181:** © chris mcloughlin/Alam **p182:** Caspar Benson/Getty Images; **p184:** © David J. Green/Alamy; **p187:** © Elmtree Images/Alamy **p188:** Jannis Tobias Werner/Shutterstock; **p192-193:** © Mike Goldwater/Alamy; **p195:** PhilAugusta iStockphoto; **p196:** © incamerastock/Alamy; **p200:** Vasily Smirnov/Shutterstock

Designed by Kamae Design

Although we have made every effort to trace and contact all copyright holders before publication t has not been possible in all cases. If notified, the publisher will rectify any errors or omissions at th earliest opportunity.